THE NATIONAL TRUST BOOK OF
Christmas & Festive Day Recipes

Sara Paston-Williams

DAVID & CHARLES
Newton Abbot   London   North Pomfret (Vt)

QUANTITIES AND CONVERSIONS

In all the following recipes the approximate metric equivalents have been given in brackets after the imperial measure, eg 1 lb (450 g) plain flour. Although not exact—1 lb in fact equals 453.6 g—these equivalents are accurate enough for practical cookery purposes, as grams and millilitres are so small that plus or minus five makes very little difference.

The metric abbreviations used are: g = gram; kg = kilogram; ml = millilitre. A teaspoon is equivalent in metric terms to 5 ml; a tablespoon to 15 ml.

For American readers: 1 tbsp = 1$\frac{1}{4}$ US tbsp; 2 tbsp = 3 US tbsp; 1 pt = 2$\frac{1}{2}$ US cups; 1 dessertspoon = about 1 US tbsp. The Imperial pint is 20 fl oz whereas the US pint is 16 fl oz.

British Library Cataloguing in Publication Data

Paston-Williams, Sara
    The National Trust book of Christmas and festive day recipes
    1. Cookery
    2. Festivals
    I. Title
    641.5′68   TX739

    ISBN 0-7153-8100-8

    Library of Congress Catalog Card Number: 80-85514

Typeset by ABM Typographics Limited, Hull
and printed in Great Britain
by Redwood Burn Limited, Trowbridge, Wiltshire
for David & Charles (Publishers) Limited
Brunel House   Newton Abbot   Devon

Published in the United States of America
by David & Charles Inc
North Pomfret   Vermont 05053   USA

CONTENTS

For my family and other friends

Grateful thanks to my husband
for his tasting and helpful criticism,
and to Pat Richards
for typing the manuscript.

Thanks also to the
Brotherton Library at the University of Leeds
for letting me look at
their marvellous collection of old recipe books,
and to
my family and many friends
who gave me their favourite recipes.

INTRODUCTION

In days gone by, the whole Christian year was a cycle of religious feasts. Many of these festivals may be traced back to pre-Christian practices. In ancient Scandinavia, where we find the origins of so many English customs, a most magnificent festival in honour of the god Thor started the winter solstice, called Mother Night. The festival was dominated by Yule or Yeol. When Christianity superseded the rites of pagan worship, the Anglo-Saxons expressed the greatest reluctance to relinquish this annual rejoicing, and so, to ensure success to their preaching, the missionaries applied the festival to the Nativity of Christ, which acquired the name Yule-Feast. The peace-offerings dedicated to Thor were cakes of fine flour sweetened with honey—perhaps ancestors of our Yule-Cake. It has been suggested that the practice of pouring spirit over the Christmas pudding and setting it alight is a relic of the fire worship with which our ancestors celebrated this festival.

Easter is another of our religious festivals, said to date back to a feast held in the spring for Eostre, the goddess of the dawn and spring; many of our Easter customs are pagan in origin. The forerunners of our Hot Cross Buns were believed to have been eaten at this spring festival when their roundness was said to depict the sun and the fire, and their cross, the seasons. Of course, in order to make Hot Cross Buns acceptable when Christianity was introduced, the cross became the symbolic Cross of Christ. Hard-boiled eggs were also associated with pre-Christian rites at the great spring festival. They were thought to be emblems of the regeneration of mankind. Any present-day festivals involving the lighting of bonfires can be traced back to pre-Christian times, when fire was worshipped and bonfires were lit as protection from evil spirits.

The non-festal period in the Church between Whitsuntide and Christmas was convenient for local celebrations with much feasting. Most villages had their own feast days to celebrate a successful local harvest such as a Cherry-Pie or Strawberry Feast, and the local squire would usually hold a feast for his tenants to celebrate a marriage or coming-of-age in his family. Other feast days developed around the collecting of farm rents on Ladyday and Michaelmas.

The festive fare really depended on what was around at the time of the feasting, and over the years the fare became traditional and was passed down from generation to generation. Nowadays, in Britain, we have few feast days which seems a shame. Our ancestors appear to have staggered from one feast to the next and I am sure we are missing something! Perhaps you would like to reintroduce some of these feast days into your life; so here are some recipes, which I hope you will enjoy reading about—and cooking!

An English Christmas Home!

CHRISTMAS

'Many, merry Christmasses, many happy New Years, unbroken friendships, great accumulation of cheerful recollections, affection on earth, and heaven at last.'

Christmas, as we know it, was really started by the Victorians. It was the festivities of the Royal Family that were the people's model. Christmas cards were invented and candle-lit Christmas trees were popularised by Prince Albert, as was the Christmas Plum Pudding. The snow-white, iced and decorated Christmas Cake was also a Victorian innovation and, indeed, Father Christmas himself arrived in Victorian times.

Before this, Yule-tide feasts and entertainments were enjoyed only by the wealthy. The medieval and Elizabethan feasts of goose and great sides of roast beef took place in the baronial halls; the majority of people enjoyed no festivities until greater prosperity enabled them to celebrate Christmas. So here are some of my favourite recipes to help you do just that. I have started with a few warming drinks to offer guests or carol singers on Christmas Eve and to put you in the festive mood.

Hot Christmas Punch (*serves 8*)
Church wakes or festivals have been occasions for indulgence since medieval times. Ale was the most popular drink then, and there were Easter-ales, Whitsun-ales, Midsummer-ales, and Christmas-ales. Spiced ales and wines were also popular.

12 lumps sugar	4 tablespoons water
2 oranges	2 lemons
8 cloves	1 bottle (litre) cider
1 level teaspoon ground nutmeg	1 sherry glass rum
1 stick cinnamon	1 sherry glass brandy

Rub sugar lumps over rind of 1 orange to remove zest. Cut this orange in half, squeeze out juice and put into pan with sugar. Cut second orange into 8 sections, stick a clove into skin of each section and then sprinkle with nutmeg. Add to pan with cinnamon, water and rind of lemons cut into strips. Heat gently until sugar dissolves and then simmer for 5 minutes. Leave to cool until needed.

Remove cinnamon stick, pour in cider and heat until really hot, but not boiling. Pour into serving bowl. Heat rum and brandy very gently in a small saucepan, ignite with a match, and while flaming pour into the punch mixture. Serve immediately.

Lamb's Wool

This is a version of mulled ale made with sugar, spices and the pulp of roasted apples. For many centuries the apple has been an important feature of Christmas. If the sun shone through the branches of the apple trees on Christmas morning it was a sign of a good crop to come. Also, if the trees were covered with snow this meant they would be covered with fruit at harvest-time. Originally it was the wild crab apples that were mainly available to the country folk. These were served in hot drinks and punches. On Christmas morning, farm and estate labourers were invited 'up to the House' with their wives and offered Lamb's Wool and the best cider to drink. It was also a traditional drink for Christmas Eve, served with 'Wigs' or Spiced Yule Bread (see recipes on pages 9-10).

4 large eating apples	$\frac{1}{2}$ teaspoon nutmeg
2 pt (1·25 l) brown ale	$\frac{1}{2}$ teaspoon ginger
1 pt (500 ml) sweet white wine	Thin strip of lemon rind
3 in (7·5 cm) cinnamon stick	Soft dark brown sugar to taste

Slit skin round centre of each apple. (You can use crab apples if you have them.) Bake in oven at 350°F (180°C) Gas Mark 4 until soft and pulpy.

Heat brown ale, wine, spices and lemon rind in a large saucepan. Remove apple flesh from skins and mash. Stir into liquid. Remove cinnamon stick and lemon rind, then pass the mixture through a sieve pressing down well. Reheat, adding brown sugar to taste.

Serve steaming from a punch bowl, into earthenware mugs or glass tankards.

Mulled Port

This drink is called 'Bishop' and was named by Oxford and Cambridge undergraduates. In Northern Europe, 'Bischop' refers to any hot, spiced wine.

1 orange (stuck with 6 cloves)	Sugar to taste
1 bottle Ruby port	½ pt (250 ml) water (optional)

Cut orange in half, and place in a stainless steel pan with port and a little sugar. (Some people prefer this drink without sugar.) Heat gently and when at simmering point, set alight and allow it to burn for a few seconds. Pour into a warmed punch bowl. Dilute with water if you wish. Serve immediately with a ladle into warmed port glasses.

Mulled Red Wine

This mulled wine is certainly the warmest and most friendly of Christmas drinks. It is not expensive and is ideal to serve on a cold night to unexpected visitors or carol singers. To save complicated last-minute preparations, it is a good idea to make the spicy syrup base a day or two in advance. It can then be heated and the wine added when required.

2 bottles red wine

FOR SYRUP BASE:

6 large oranges	1 teaspoon ground nutmeg
8 oz (225 g) granulated sugar	1 dessertspoon whole cloves
1 teaspoon ground cinnamon	3 pt (1·75 l) water

Roughly cut up the oranges and place these in a pan with all the other ingredients including the water. Bring to the boil and then simmer gently for about 30 minutes without a lid. Strain through a fine sieve. Your syrup is now made and can be kept in the refrigerator until required.

When you want to serve your mulled wine, first bring the syrup to the boil in a large pan then add the two bottles of red wine—the cheapest will do. Warm up again, but do not boil. Serve in glasses which have been previously warmed.

(Note: The quantities of spices may be varied to suit individual tastes. The wine does not have to be of good quality—add more or less wine to suit your palate. Experiment a week or so before Christmas to make sure the seasonal spirit of goodwill begins early.)

Christmas Eve Wigs (makes 6–8 cakes)

'Wigs' were small cakes of spiced dough offered to guests on Christmas Eve. They were dipped in mulled ale or mulled elderberry wine, and eaten instead of mince pies.

3 oz (75 g) butter	2 teaspoons caraway seeds
8 oz (225 g) self-raising flour	1 egg, beaten
1 oz (25 g) caster sugar	A little milk to mix
1 oz (25 g) candied peel, chopped	

Pre-set oven at 425°F (220°C) Gas Mark 7.

Rub butter into flour, add sugar, chopped peel and caraway seeds. Mix to a soft dough with beaten egg and a little milk. Put into greased bun tins and bake in pre-heated oven for about 20 minutes until golden brown. Eat with Lamb's Wool or Mulled Red Wine (see recipes on pages 8 and 9).

'Wigs' were also eaten at Lent. The caraway seeds were said to aid digestion.

piced Yule Bread (*makes 2 lb [900 g] loaf*)

ule Bread was served to casual callers over the Christmas period th chunks of cheese and warming mulled ale. It was extremely pular in the North of England.

1 lb (450 g) plain flour	4 oz (125 g) raisins
Pinch of salt	1 tablespoon candied peel,
2 teaspoons mixed spice	chopped
2 oz (50 g) butter	1 egg
2 oz (50 g) lard	¾ oz (22 g) fresh yeast
4 oz (125 g) sugar	1 teaspoon sugar
4 oz (125 g) currants	Warm milk for mixing

Sieve flour, salt and spices together in a bowl. Rub in butter and lard. Mix in sugar, dried fruit and peel. Add lightly beaten egg. Cream together yeast and sugar with a little warm milk. Add this to the mixture with sufficient warm milk to make a not too sticky dough. Cover with a cloth and leave in a warm place to rise until doubled in bulk. Knead on a floured board and then put in a greased 2 lb (900 g) loaf tin. Leave to prove for another 15 minutes.

Meanwhile pre-set oven to 400°F (200°C) Gas Mark 6. Bake the Yule Bread for about 1 hour. Remove when evenly brown and risen. Cool on a wire rack.

Serve thickly sliced with or without butter. Try serving it with Lamb's Wool, Mulled Red Wine (see recipes, pages 8 and 9) or cider—especially good late on Christmas Eve when your spirits are beginning to flag.

Almond Soup (*serves 6*)

Almonds, like chestnuts, were once used much more in cooking than they are now. They are expensive, but why not treat the family to this delicate and unusual soup over the Christmas holiday.

4 oz (125 g) ground almonds	Salt
½ pt (250 ml) milk	Pinch of mace
2 tablespoons fresh white breadcrumbs	Pinch of cayenne pepper
	½ pt (250 ml) single cream
1 oz (25 g) butter	A few flaked almonds
1 oz (25 g) flour	1 tablespoon melted butter
2 pt (1·25 l) chicken stock	

Put the ground almonds into a small saucepan with the milk. Simmer gently for 10 minutes. Add the breadcrumbs and simmer for a further 3 minutes. Liquidise in a blender or rub through a sieve. In a large pan, melt the butter, add the flour, stir and cook for a few seconds. Stir in the almond purée. Gradually add the stock and when you have a smooth soup, season with salt, cayenne pepper and mace.

Simmer slowly for 10 minutes and then remove from the heat and stir in the cream. Heat through again gently. Meanwhile, fry the flaked almonds in the butter until golden brown. Scatter them over the soup just before serving and sprinkle with finely chopped parsley. Serve with extra fried almonds in a small bowl on the table.

Brussels Sprout and Hazelnut Soup (*serves 6*)
This is an unusual combination of ingredients, but sprouts do marry very well with most kinds of nuts. The secret is not to overcook this soup or it will lose its colour.

8 oz (225 g) onions, chopped	2 bay leaves
2 oz (50 g) butter	1 oz (25 g) plain flour
1 lb (450 g) fresh Brussels sprouts, roughly chopped	1½ pt (750 ml) chicken stock
	Salt
4 oz (125 g) hazelnuts, chopped	Freshly milled black pepper

Melt butter in a large saucepan and add chopped onion. Cook for a few minutes to soften onion, but do not let it brown. Add chopped Brussels sprouts, hazelnuts and bay leaves, cover with a piece of greaseproof paper and saucepan lid, and leave to 'sweat' over a very low heat. After a few minutes, check that vegetables are nice and buttery and softened, then add flour and stir, followed by chicken stock.

Bring to the boil slowly, stirring frequently to blend in the stock.

Simmer until the sprouts are just tender. Pass through a sieve or mouli, or liquidise in a blender until smooth. Season with salt and pepper to taste.

Serve piping hot with a swirl of cream and a separate bowl of hot roasted hazelnuts to accompany it.

Chestnut Soup *(serves 6)*

This is a very rich and delicious soup ideal for serving on Boxing Day with the cold turkey and ham. It can be made 2 or 3 days before Christmas and kept in the refrigerator. It also freezes very well.

1 lb (450 g) fresh chestnuts
1 rasher good-flavoured
  green bacon (optional)
1 oz (25 g) butter
2 oz (50 g) onions
1 stick of celery
3 oz (75 g) carrot
2 oz (50 g) potato
1½ pt (750 ml) chicken or veal stock

½ teacup dry Madeira (optional)
Salt
Freshly ground black pepper
¼ level teaspoon powdered mace
Pinch of sugar
2 tablespoons double cream
Crisply fried bacon rolls and
  sippets to garnish

Make a slit in each chestnut and drop into boiling water for 10 minutes. Remove the outer and inner skins. If including the bacon, de-rind the rasher and cut into strips—some people don't like its rather over-powering flavour in soup, although I think it goes particularly well with the chestnuts here. Melt butter in a saucepan and fry bacon strips until crisp. Chop onion roughly and add to bacon (just soften the onion in the butter if you decide not to use bacon). Add celery, carrot and potato cut into even-sized pieces. Fry these for a few minutes. Add peeled chestnuts and toss in pan. Cover with cold stock. Bring to boil, cover and simmer until chestnuts are tender. This will take approx 1½ hours.

Pass soup through a mouli or sieve or put into a blender. Add the Madeira, if you are using it. Taste and adjust the seasoning with salt, pepper, mace and sugar. If the soup is too thick, add extra stock.

Reheat and stir in the cream just before serving. Garnish with tiny crisply fried rolls of bacon and sippets (small cubes or triangles) of fried bread.

Stilton Soup *(serves 6)*

This is an ideal soup to make towards the end of the festive season, using up odd pieces of Stilton.

2 oz (50 g) butter
1 onion, finely chopped
2 sticks celery, chopped
1½ oz (40 g) plain flour
3 tablespoons dry white
  wine
1½ pt (750 ml) chicken or
  veal stock

½ pt (250 ml) milk
4 oz (125 g) Stilton cheese,
  mashed or grated
2 oz (50 g) strong Cheddar or
  Gruyère cheese, grated
Salt
Freshly milled white pepper
4 tablespoons double cream

12

Melt butter in a heavy-based saucepan and add the vegetables. Cover the vegetables with a sheet of greaseproof paper and the saucepan lid and leave to 'sweat' for 5 minutes. Stir in flour and cook gently for a few seconds. Remove from the heat and stir in wine and stock. Return to heat and stir until mixture reaches boiling point. Simmer for 30 minutes, or until wine has lost its harsh taste.

Add the milk and the cheese. Stir until just below boiling point. Add salt and freshly milled pepper to taste. Pass the soup through a mouli or sieve, or liquidise in a blender. Reheat the soup without boiling. Just before serving, add the cream and garnish with sippets of fried bread and chopped parsley.

Tomato, Apple and Celery Soup *(serves 4–6)*
This is a very Christmassy soup.

2 oz (50 g) butter	6 oz (175 g) apples,
4 oz (125 g) onions, finely	quartered
chopped	$\frac{1}{4}$ teaspoon salt
6 oz (175 g) tomatoes,	Freshly milled black pepper
quartered	Freshly grated nutmeg
6 oz (175 g) celery, cut in	1 small pinch ground ginger
2 in (5 cm) lengths	1 pt (500 ml) chicken or
$2\frac{1}{2}$ fl oz (60 ml) dry sherry	turkey stock

FOR GARNISH:
Apple slices	Fresh chives, chopped

Melt butter in a large pan and add onions. Cook gently for 10 minutes or until onions are golden brown. Add other vegetables, apples, sherry, seasoning and spices to pan. Cover with greaseproof paper and lid of pan and 'sweat' by simmering gently for 10 minutes until all vegetables are nice and buttery.

Add stock to contents of pan, replace saucepan lid and simmer gently again until vegetables and fruit are tender. Pass soup through blender and finally through a sieve to remove any remaining pips or stalks. Return to clean pan and reheat. Taste and adjust seasoning. Serve in warmed soup bowls and garnish with chopped chives and apple slices. Accompany with a bowl of croutons.

Honey and Mustard Roast Pork
If you feel like ringing the changes, a splendid leg of home-produced pork is as traditional at Christmas as Roast Turkey or Goose. It can also be a good buy. Of course if you are having a large number sitting around the Christmas table for lunch, serve this Roast Pork alongside the Turkey and have a 'greate feaste'! (Roast chicken and pork were often found together at medieval feasts.)

This is an old recipe where the joint is prepared and left overnight in its coat of honey, mustard and spices. Any meat left over is really excellent cold, served with Cranberry and Apple Relish (page 15), Spiced Prunes (page 25) or Spiced Orange Rings (page 24).

6–8 lb (2·8–3·6 kg) leg of pork
1 garlic clove
5 level tablespoons
  Dijon mustard
5 level tablespoons
  thick honey

2 tablespoons cooking oil
Pinch of thyme, marjoram and
  sage
Pinch of ginger
Salt
Freshly milled black pepper

On Christmas Eve, remove rind from pork with a small sharp knife and reserve. Place joint in a large roasting tin lined with foil—a piece large enough to loosely wrap joint next day. Rub the flesh with clove of garlic. Combine mustard, honey, oil, herbs and ginger. Season with plenty of pepper and smear all over joint.

Next day, when you are ready to cook the meat, wrap foil over joint and roast at 375°F (190°C) Gas Mark 4 for 35 minutes per 1 lb (450 g) plus an extra 25 minutes. Open up foil for the last 35 minutes of cooking time, baste joint and leave to brown.

Meanwhile cut pork rind into fine strips with kitchen scissors or a sharp knife. Place in a tin, brush over with oil, sprinkle with salt and cook in oven with joint for about 1½ hours or until crisp.

Serve Roast Leg of Pork on a large meat platter together with the crackling. Surrounded with Apricot Stuffing Balls (see below) or Apple, Onion and Sage Stuffing Balls (page 106) or serve with Baked Apples stuffed with Apricots (page 110), or Prune and Apple Sauce (page 109).

Apricot Stuffing Balls (makes 12 balls)

4 oz (125 g) dried apricots,
  soaked overnight
4 oz (125 g) celery, finely
  chopped
6 oz (175 g) fresh white
  breadcrumbs
½ level teaspoon dried sage

¼ level teaspoon mixed spice
1 oz (25 g) melted butter
Salt
Freshly milled black pepper
1 small egg
1 level tablespoon Dijon
  mustard

Drain apricots and chop. Combine these with celery, breadcrumbs, sage, spice, butter and plenty of seasoning, in a bowl. Beat egg and mustard together and use to bind stuffing. If necessary, moisten with a little stock. Shape into 12 balls and roll in a little flour.

One hour before the pork is due to be cooked, open up foil and arrange stuffing balls around the joint. Return to oven to finish cooking. These stuffing balls can be prepared the day before, and kept in the refrigerator overnight.

Cranberry and Apple Relish

Serve this delicious relish with hot or cold roast pork, ham or turkey. It will keep for at least a week in the refrigerator or can be frozen.

8 oz (225 g) cranberries
12 oz (350 g) cooking apples
2 tablespoons cider vinegar

8 oz (225 g) soft brown sugar
½ level teaspoon mixed spice
Grated rind of 1 orange

Wash cranberries and put in a saucepan. Peel, core and slice apples and add to pan with vinegar, sugar and spice. Add grated orange rind. Cook over medium heat, stirring occasionally, for about 20 minutes or until fruit is pulpy. Add 4 tablespoons water and continue cooking for 2–3 minutes. Cool, and use as required.

Traditional Roast Turkey

Everybody knows the old Christmas song in which the true love gives his lady a 'partridge in a pear tree'; what they may not know is that the birds mentioned were traditional Christmas presents all destined to end up on the table! The turkey was brought back to Britain from Central America, where it was already domesticated, by early explorers about 1523. It grew in popularity in England and soon became a farmyard fowl replacing the old celebratory birds such as swans, geese and doves.

Before the railways were developed, large flocks of turkeys were brought to the London market from Cambridgeshire, Suffolk and Norfolk on foot, beginning their journey in August at the end of the harvest.

Norfolk turkeys are still famous, but they all need careful cooking or the meat can be dry and indigestible. Stuffings are very important to keep the turkey moist and add flavour. These used to be tremendously rich and spicy—oysters, chestnuts, saffron, prunes, cinnamon, port, oranges, lemons, cloves and anchovies were all used. Fruit sauces, such as cranberry, redcurrant, bilberry and rowanberry, were as popular an accompaniment as they are now, and succulent pork sausages were essential. A Victorian habit was to leave the sausages in strings and festoon them around the bird like an alderman's chains just before it was carried triumphantly to the table. This looks marvellous—try it!

There are many ways of cooking turkey, but here is the one I have found most successful. I don't use cooking foil as to me this gives a rather stewed taste to the bird. The advantages of slow over quick roasting are debatable. Quick cooking seals the bird and gives better flavour, while the slower method reduces shrinkage. The best compromise is to put the bird into a hot oven to start with and then reduce the heat for most of the cooking time.

15–20 lb (6–9 kg) fresh hen turkey	Salt
2 types of prepared stuffing	Freshly milled black pepper
Melted butter	Fatty rashers of green bacon
	Piece of muslin soaked in butter

If you are using a frozen bird, do allow adequate time for thawing—at least 3 days. It is extremely dangerous to cook any poultry which has not been completely thawed out. Also make sure that your thawed turkey has a dry skin, or it will never crisp up properly.

The sinews and strings *should* be drawn from the legs—perhaps your butcher will do this for you. Prepare your chosen stuffings—try to get variety in colour and flavour (see recipes on pages 17–19). Don't stuff the bird until Christmas morning or the day on which you are going to roast it, as fresh air should always be able to circulate within the carcass. Loosen neck skin and push one of the stuffings well into breast cavity. Pull skin gently over stuffing and fasten under wing tips—a skewer can be used to hold it firm. Put second stuffing into carcass through vent end, being careful not to pack too tightly or it will not cook through. Retie trussing string. Place turkey on a wire rack in a large roasting tin. Prick breast all over with a fine skewer or sharp cocktail stick to help prevent skin bursting during cooking. Brush all over generously with melted butter. Season with salt and black pepper. Cover breast with fat bacon.

Place in pre-heated oven at 425°F (220°C) Gas Mark 7 and cook for 45 minutes, basting every 20 minutes. Reduce oven heat to 325°F (170°C) Gas Mark 4 for a further 4–5 hours depending on size of turkey. After 1 hour of cooking, cut the trussing string around the drumsticks, (they should be set by this time) so that the heat circulates. At the same time, cover the breast with a piece of clean muslin or cloth soaked in melted butter, to add extra protection. Baste frequently.

After 4 or 5 hours, put oven up to 400°F (200°C) Gas Mark 6 and cook for a further 40 minutes, protecting drumsticks with cloth if they are getting too brown. Remove bacon and cloth from breast for the final 15 minutes so that it can brown and become crisp.

Test with a fine skewer inserted into thickest part of thigh to see if turkey is cooked—clear juice should run out. If it is the slightest bit pink, continue cooking.

When turkey is cooked, remove from oven and allow to settle for 15 minutes before carving—it will carve much better if you do this, and it also allows you time to make the gravy and bacon rolls, etc!

Serve on a large meat platter surrounded by bacon rolls, or Bacon and Chestnut Rolls (see recipe on page 20), lovely brown pork sausages, and garnished with watercress or parsley. Make frills for

16

the drumsticks (the same way as I describe for a ham frill in the recipe for Christmas Baked Ham (page 22). Serve accompanied by Chestnut Purée (page 21), or Hot Spiced Chestnuts and Prunes (page 22), Bread Sauce (page 20) or Cranberry, Orange and Port Sauce (page 21).

Medieval Endoring or Gilding

This process was used to give roast poultry a gilded or 'endored' appearance. It really does make the Christmas bird look splendid.

1 oz (25 g) butter	2 tablespoons white wine
$\frac{1}{4}$ teaspoon saffron	vinegar
1 oz (25 g) sugar	1 egg yolk

Cook butter with saffron very gently until butter has turned bright yellow. Strain to remove saffron strands. Return to pan and add sugar and vinegar. Cook until syrupy. Remove from heat and stir in egg yolk. Continue cooking, without boiling, until thick. 10 minutes before your bird is cooked, remove from oven and paint it with gilding mixture. Return to oven and continue cooking.

Cooking Times for different-sized Turkeys

(1) 8–10 lb (3·6–4·5 kg) oven-ready weight
30 minutes at oven temperature 425°F (220°C) Gas Mark 7, then $2\frac{1}{2}$–3 hours at oven temperature 325°F (170°C) Gas Mark 3, then 30 minutes at oven temperature 400°F (200°C) Gas Mark 6.
(2) 10–15 lb (4·5–6·7 kg) oven-ready weight
40 minutes at oven temperature 425°F (220°C) Gas Mark 7, then 3–$3\frac{1}{2}$ hours at oven temperature 325°F (170°C) Gas Mark 3, then 45 minutes at oven temperature 400°F (200°C) Gas Mark 6.

Bacon and Herb Stuffing

4 oz (125 g) smoked bacon rashers	1 tablespoon fresh parsley, chopped
2 oz (50 g) butter	4 oz (125 g) shredded butcher's suet
1 medium-sized onion, chopped	8 oz (225 g) fresh white breadcrumbs
1 tablespoon fresh lemon thyme and basil, chopped (or 2 teaspoons mixed herbs)	Salt
	Freshly milled black pepper
	1 beaten egg

Cut bacon rashers (after de-rinding) into strips and fry these in butter until golden brown. Add chopped onion and fry until soft and transparent. Mix herbs together with suet and breadcrumbs in a basin. Add contents of pan to the basin, season well and bind with beaten egg.

Brazil Nut Stuffing

16 slices white bread
1 lb (450 g) Brazil nuts,
  finely chopped
2 medium-sized onions,
  finely chopped
1 large stick celery,
  chopped

2 teaspoons salt
Freshly milled black pepper
$\frac{3}{4}$ pt (400 ml) giblet stock
4 oz (125 g) butter
2 tablespoons brandy
4 tablespoons fresh parsley,
  chopped

Remove crusts from slices of bread and cut into $\frac{1}{2}$ in (1 cm) squares and place in a bowl. Add nuts, onion and celery, mix well together and season with salt and pepper. Heat giblet stock and add butter. Pour stock over bread mixture. Stir in brandy and parsley. Leave in a cool place for several hours, preferably overnight, before stuffing the turkey.

Chestnut Stuffing

12 chestnuts
Stock
1 oz (25 g) butter
1 turkey liver, chopped
4 oz (125 g) fresh white
  breadcrumbs

3 inner sticks celery, chopped
$\frac{1}{4}$ pt (150 ml) milk
4 sprigs fresh parsley, chopped
Salt
Freshly milled black pepper

Make a slit in chestnuts, cover with boiling water for 10 minutes, and remove outer and inner skins. Put skinned chestnuts in a pan with stock to cover, bring to boil and simmer until tender, about 30 minutes.

Melt butter and fry turkey liver. Mix this with breadcrumbs, celery, milk and the roughly chopped chestnuts. Stir in parsley and season to taste. The stuffing is now ready to use.

Dried Apricot and Almond Stuffing

8 oz (225 g) dried apricots
1 large onion, chopped
2 oz (50 g) butter
2 oz (50 g) blanched almonds,
  chopped
4 oz (125 g) seedless raisins
4 oz (125 g) fresh white
  breadcrumbs

1 teaspoon grated orange rind
1 level teaspoon allspice
2 tablespoons sweet sherry or
  Madeira
1 teaspoon brown sugar
Salt
Freshly milled black pepper

Cover dried apricots with water and leave to soak overnight. (Be careful not to buy very cheap apricots, they tend to have an ammonia flavour.)

Next day, fry onion gently in butter until softened and golden brown. Strain apricots and chop into small pieces. Mix all ingredients together into a loose stuffing and place in turkey.

My Mother's Sausagemeat and Mushroom Stuffing

¼ pt (150 ml) milk
6 cloves
1 bayleaf
1 medium-sized onion, chopped
1 lb (450 g) good quality pork sausagemeat

4 oz (125 g) button mushrooms, chopped
4 oz (125 g) fresh white breadcrumbs
1 tablespoon fresh sage, finely chopped (or 2 teaspoons dried sage)
1 egg, separated

Put milk into a saucepan with cloves, bayleaf and chopped onion. Bring to boil and remove from heat. Allow to stand for 10 minutes. Remove cloves and bayleaf.

Meanwhile, break up sausagemeat and fry gently without adding any fat. Remove to a mixing bowl when golden brown and cooked through, leaving fat from sausagemeat in pan. Fry mushrooms very gently in the remaining fat, then add to bowl.

Add breadcrumbs and herbs to sausagemeat and mushroom mixture. Stir in milk and onion mixture. Add egg yolk and thoroughly combine all ingredients together. Leave for at least an hour in a cold place.

Just before using the stuffing, fold in a stiffly beaten egg white. This helps to keep it light and moist.

Smoked Ham and Almond Stuffing

4 oz (125 g) butter
2 onions, finely chopped
8 oz (225 g) smoked ham, minced
4 oz (125 g) fresh breadcrumbs
4 tablespoons chopped parsley

½ teaspoon dried thyme
4 tablespoons dry red wine
2 eggs
3 oz (75 g) blanched almonds, chopped
Salt
Freshly ground black pepper

Melt the butter in a frying pan. Add the onions and fry until softened. Remove from the heat and stir in the ham and breadcrumbs, followed by the remaining ingredients. Season with salt and pepper.

Whisky Gravy (*serves 6–8*)

BASIC TURKEY STOCK:

Turkey giblets, except the liver
3 pt (1·75 l) water
1 carrot, chopped
1 onion, quartered

2 blades mace
6 peppercorns
Bunch of herbs

Place all ingredients in a saucepan and simmer together for 2 hours. These quantities will make 1–1½ pt (500–750 ml) of stock. This can be prepared on Christmas Eve, so that it is available for making the gravy once the turkey is cooked.

GRAVY:

1–1½ pt (500–750 ml) turkey
   stock, strained
1 small glass Scotch whisky
1 oz (25 g) plain flour

Salt
Freshly ground black pepper
¼ pt (150 ml) double cream

When turkey is cooked, place it on a meat dish and spoon out all but 1 tablespoon of fat from roasting tin. Pour in whisky and boil furiously on top of stove for 2 minutes. Now stir in flour and scrape tin to release sediment of cooking juices. Cook for a few minutes, then remove from heat and gradually add stock stirring all the time. Return to heat and cook until thick and smooth stirring continuously. Season. Just before serving, pour in the cream and stir until smooth. Taste and season again if necessary.

Bacon and Chestnut Rolls (*serves 8*)

These are just a little bit different from the plain bacon rolls that are traditionally served with roast turkey. Try them for a change with roast chicken at other times of the year. You can use tinned chestnuts, if you can't buy fresh.

6 oz (175 g) streaky bacon
1 lb (450 g) cooked fresh chestnuts

Remove rind from bacon and stretch each rasher with back of a knife. Cut each rasher into 2 pieces and roll each piece round a cooked chestnut. Thread rolls carefully on to skewers and grill for 5 minutes or until golden brown. Serve immediately, placed around the turkey.

(Note: These rolls can be cooked earlier and reheated for a few seconds under the grill just before serving.)

Bread Sauce (*serves 6–8*)

This is a very smooth bread sauce and very different from the stodgy disaster too often served with roast turkey or chicken in many restaurants today. It is passed through a blender or hair sieve, and flavoured with spices and herbs.

½ pt (250 ml) milk or chicken stock
2 oz (50 g) butter
1 small onion, roughly chopped
½ clove garlic, crushed
1 bayleaf
1 teaspoon dried sage
1 blade of mace, or a little nutmeg, or 2 cloves
3 oz (75 g) fresh white breadcrumbs
¼ pt (150 ml) single cream
Salt
Freshly ground white pepper

Put milk or stock, butter, onion, garlic, bayleaf, sage and mace or cloves or nutmeg into top of a double saucepan or into a basin over a saucepan of boiling water. Heat mixture until hot but not boiling. Add breadcrumbs and let sauce cook until it is quite thick and smooth. Remove bayleaf and mace or cloves and pass sauce through a blender or hair sieve.

Add cream, adjust seasoning, and reheat. If sauce is too thick (this will depend on the kind of bread you have used) add a little more milk or stock. If you have to keep the sauce hot, return it to double saucepan after sieving and cover with a circle of buttered greaseproof paper to prevent a skin forming. (You can use this method with any sauce or custard that you want to keep warm.) Serve sauce when you are ready. It looks most attractive served in bouchée (little vol-au-vent) cases around the turkey.

Chestnut Purée

The Christmas turkey is not complete for me without this delicious purée.

2 lb (900 g) fresh chestnuts
1 oz (25 g) butter
½ onion, finely chopped
Salt
Freshly ground pepper
¼ pt (150 ml) double cream

Slit chestnuts with a sharp knife on flat side and boil in water for 30 minutes. Remove outer and inner skins and mash. Push through a sieve or liquidise in a blender. Melt butter in saucepan and cook onion until soft and transparent. Add chestnut purée. Season to taste and add cream. Serve hot or cold.

Cranberry, Orange and Port Sauce (serves 8)

Traditionally this is served with roast turkey, but it is also delicious with roast pork. Serve as an alternative to bread or apple sauce, or in addition. The sweetness of the sauce complements the bland flavour of turkey or the richness of pork. It looks most attractive if served in fresh orange shells all around the Christmas turkey. Also it can be made well in advance and frozen.

8 oz (225 g) fresh or frozen cranberries
Grated rind and juice of 1 orange
¼ pt (150 ml) water
4 oz (125 g) granulated sugar
1 tablespoon port

21

Wash cranberries and place in a pan with all other ingredients. Bring to boil slowly. Simmer uncovered until tender, about 10 minutes, bruising cranberries with a wooden spoon. Pour into a jar or container, cool, cover and store in refrigerator for up to a week. Freeze at this point if wished. To serve, pile into attractive sauce boat or serve in fresh V-shaped orange shells placed around the turkey.

Hot Spiced Chestnuts and Prunes *(serves 6)*

Try this recipe as an accompaniment to roast turkey. Prunes and chestnuts were two ingredients used in the past to stuff all types of poultry. Their richness is a good contrast to the more bland taste of turkey meat.

12 oz (350 g) dried prunes	1 tablespoon caster sugar
Cold tea	1 teaspoon ground cinnamon
1 lb (450 g) fresh chestnuts	Pinch of salt
1 pt (500 ml) chicken or	1 teaspoon lemon juice
turkey stock	1 wineglass sherry

Soak prunes in cold tea overnight. Slit chestnuts on flat side with a sharp knife and drop into a pan of boiling water. Boil for 5 minutes and taking a few at a time, remove outer and inner skins. Now put back into a saucepan with stock, add salt and simmer until tender, about 30 minutes.

Meanwhile, poach prunes in soaking liquor, sweetened with caster sugar and spiced with cinnamon. After 15 minutes when plump and just tender, drain and reserve juice.

Mix prunes with chestnuts and moisten with wineglass of prune juice, lemon juice and wineglass of sherry. Heat through and serve in a tureen.

Christmas Baked Ham

Many people consider ham an essential part of the Christmas festivities, and indeed it always has been—the family pig was fattened up for Christmas. Ham is a splendid joint for the cold table and provides a delicious meal for any unexpected guests—it also makes a very easy breakfast for Christmas morning.

This old-fashioned way of baking ham in a flour and water or 'huff' paste dates back to medieval times. The juices and flavour are completely sealed in the paste case and the ham remains moist, full of flavour and shrinks less. It can be finished off with a variety of glazes or coatings, some of which I have suggested after this recipe. (You can use a double layer of aluminium cooking foil in place of the 'huff' paste if you want, but you won't get quite such a good result.)

22

10–14 lb (4·5—6 kg) ham
Cloves

FOR FLOUR AND WATER PASTE:
3 lb (1·4 kg) plain flour
1½ pt (750 ml) water

Scrape ham well with a knife, removing any rust from underside. Soak in plenty of cold water overnight. Change water if possible. (Your butcher may tell you that nowadays hams don't need to be soaked, but I still find it necessary.) Next day, drain off water, scraping underside of ham again, and dry.

Pre-set oven at 350°F (180°C) Gas Mark 4. Make a flour and water paste, roll out on a floured board and wrap around ham. Place in a large roasting tin and bake in pre-heated oven allowing 25 minutes per 1 lb (450 g). When cooked, remove from paste case and strip off skin from ham. Score fat with a knife into diamond shapes. Insert a clove into each diamond and spread chosen glaze (see following recipes) over surface of ham. Return to oven at 375°F (190°C) Gas Mark 5 for a further 30 minutes.

Serve hot or cold and decorate as you choose. Finish off with a ham frill, which you *can* buy but is very easy to make from a piece of white cartridge paper about 8in (20cm) wide. Fold the paper in half and cut two-thirds of the way down towards the unfolded edge at ¼in (½cm) intervals. Then just wrap around the ham knuckle bone. It will look most professional. Serve with Spiced Orange Rings (page 24), Pickled Pears or Spiced Prunes (page 25) or with Cumberland Sauce (page 27).

Suggestions for Glazes:

Honey, Orange and Ginger

Mix together and spread on the ham.

3 tablespoons clear honey
3 tablespoons fresh orange juice

½ teaspoon ground ginger
1 tablespoon grated orange rind

Sugar and Spice

Mix together and sprinkle on the ham.

8 oz (225 g) Demerara sugar
1 teaspoon ground ginger

1 teaspoon mixed spice

Honey and Vinegar

Mix together and spread on the ham.

3 tablespoons clear honey

3 tablespoons wine vinegar

Honey and Mustard

Mix together and spread on the ham.

3 tablespoons clear honey or golden syrup	3 tablespoons dry English mustard

Marmalade
6 tablespoons sharp marmalade

Breadcrumbs and Sugar
Dry breadcrumbs, mixed with brown sugar and a little mace

Breadcrumbs and Parsley
Dry breadcrumbs mixed with finely chopped parsley

Oatmeal
Dredging of fine oatmeal and butter

Some suggestions for decorating ham after glazing:

Sliced bread stamped out with fancy-shaped cutters, carefully fried and used to form designs on surface of ham.

Pineapple rings with glacé cherries in their centres made to look like flowers on the ham.

Flaked and toasted almonds sprinkled all over.

Fresh orange slices in a row down centre of ham.

Fried apple rings.

Spiced Orange Rings

Oranges have been preserved in this way for centuries. They are particularly good served with cold meats, especially ham, turkey, chicken, duck and game. Home-made preserves always make popular Christmas presents too. Decorate the jars with pretty fabric tops over the vinegar-proof lids, and ribbons, pieces of holly and fancy labels. What could be a more delightful gift?

6 firm medium-sized oranges	2 teaspoons ground cloves
$\frac{3}{4}$ pt (400 ml) white vinegar	3 in piece of cinnamon stick
12 oz (350 g) granulated or soft brown sugar	$\frac{1}{2}$ level teaspoon whole cloves
	3 blades mace

Wipe oranges thoroughly. Do not peel, but cut into thin even slices approx $\frac{1}{4}$in (5mm) thick. Discard any broken slices and ends of oranges. Put in a saucepan and barely cover with water. Bring to boil, cover and simmer gently for 30–45 minutes or until peel is really tender. Drain cooking liquor into a clean pan, add vinegar, sugar and spices and heat gently until sugar has dissolved. Bring to boil and boil hard for 10 minutes. Place the well-drained orange rings, a few at a time, in syrup and simmer gently until rind becomes clear. Transfer rings straight into warmed jars, packing neatly to show shape of rings. Boil syrup again until it begins to thicken, then leave until cool but not cold. Strain and pour over oranges to cover and fill jars. Add a few whole cloves and cover with a vinegar-proof top. Store in a cool, dark place for 6–8 weeks at least, before using.

Pickled Pears
This is a delicious preserve to eat with your Christmas ham and pork, or with a slice of Stilton.

7 oz (200 g) granulated sugar	1 pt (500 ml) white wine
$\frac{1}{2}$ level tablespoon salt	vinegar
1 pt (500 ml) water	1 cinnamon stick
3 lb (1·4 kg) medium-sized	1 strip thinly pared lemon rind
hard pears	$\frac{1}{2}$ level teaspoon whole cloves

Dissolve 1 oz (25 g) of sugar and salt in water, and bring to boil. Peel, core and quarter pears and add to syrup. Bring back to boil; cover pan tightly, remove from heat and leave until cold. Put remaining sugar, vinegar, cinnamon, lemon rind and cloves into a pan. Heat until sugar dissolves then bring to boil. Drain pears very thoroughly, add to vinegar syrup and return to boil. Remove from heat then cover and leave to get cold. Boil up syrup again slowly and repeat cooling and boiling process twice more. Leave to get cold again, then pack pears into fairly small jars and cover with syrup. Do not seal jars, but top up over the next four days until no more syrup is absorbed by the fruit. Cover with a vinegar-proof lid and keep for several weeks before using.

Spiced Prunes
Prunes have long been associated with Christmas in puddings, cakes and stuffings. They were the original 'plumbs'. Instead of using them in your stuffing, try this recipe with your cold Christmas joints, particularly with cold pork. This preserve can be used 24 hours after making.

1 lb (450 g) large dried prunes	8 oz (225 g) lump sugar
2 pt (1·25 l) freshly brewed tea	Rind of 1 lemon, thinly pared
$\frac{3}{4}$ pt (400 ml) red wine vinegar	1 teaspoon pickling spice

Wash prunes and soak overnight in freshly made cold tea. Next day, put in a saucepan with half remaining soaking liquor. Cover and cook for 10–15 minutes until quite tender. Drain.

Boil vinegar, sugar, lemon rind and spices (wrapped and tied in a piece of muslin) in a pan for 5 minutes. Add ½ pt (250 ml) juice from prunes and re-boil. Remove spices and lemon rind. Put prunes into warm dry jars (you will need 2 or 3, 1 lb (450 g) jars). Pour liquor over prunes. Cover at once and store in a cool, dark place until required.

Jellied Pork Brawn (*serves 8–10*)

Brawn has been part of our traditional Christmas fare since the Middle Ages. Made from a wild boar's head and shoulders, it was richer and fattier than a ham and regarded as a delicacy for the medieval feast. In those days it was seasoned with galingale, a spicy root similar to ginger, and from this came the modern day 'galantine'. Other seasonings included grated lemon rind, mace, allspice, cloves and cayenne pepper. Very often the brawn was wrapped up in a great piece of tripe and pressed. With the decline of the wild boar, a domestic pig's head was used. The family pig was fattened up from harvest time until 'he' was killed, just before Christmas.

A cold buffet is just the answer for Christmas entertaining and this pork brawn would be a cheap but delicious addition, served with a green salad, homemade bread, and lots of spicy sauces.

½ pig's head	8 black peppercorns
12 oz (350 g) rock or sea salt	2 blades mace
1 lb (450 g) shin of beef	4 cloves
2 onions, peeled	12 whole allspice
1 bouquet garni	Juice of 1 lemon or 3 teaspoons
2 carrots sliced	white wine vinegar
2 turnips, diced	Salt
4 shallots, if available,	Freshly ground black pepper
peeled	½ teaspoon freshly grated nutmeg

Scrub the pig's half-head and put in a large pan. Cover with cold water in which the salt has been stirred. Leave to soak overnight. Next day, rinse head and barely cover with fresh cold water. Add beef, one of the onions (left whole) and the bouquet garni. Cover pan with a tightly fitting lid and bring to the boil. Simmer for 2½–3 hours, skimming occasionally, until meat is really tender, and the flesh falls from the bones.

Remove from pan and strip all meat from bones, including ear, brains and tongue. You should have about 2 lb (900 g) pig meat plus the beef. Return bones to a clean pan with cooking liquid, skimming off any fat from surface. Bring this to the boil. Add carrots, second onion, turnips, shallots, spices and lemon juice or vinegar. Tie brains in a piece of muslin and add to pan. Boil until liquid reduces to ¾ pt (400 ml). Strain and set liquid aside until cold.

Meanwhile, dice all meat finely. Skin tongue and slice thinly. Run your fingers through as you work to find any pieces of gristle or bone.

Remove solidified fat from surface of stock and strain through two thicknesses of muslin. Season lightly with salt, generously with black pepper and add ½ teaspoon of grated nutmeg. Bring back to the boil and stir in meat. Spoon brawn carefully into a large mould or basin, or two smaller containers. Make sure meat is covered with stock. Set aside in a cool place for 1 hour, then cover with a plate and leave until firmly set, preferably overnight. Turn out when required and garnish with plenty of parsley.

Serve cold, cut into fairly thick slices, with Mustard Sauce or Cumberland Sauce (see following recipes).

Mustard Sauce (*makes ½ pt (250 ml)*)
Brawn has been served with mustard sauce since Elizabethan days.

1 heaped tablespoon plain flour	2 oz (50 g) butter
1 heaped tablespoon dry mustard	½ pt (250 ml) milk, warmed
	3 tablespoons cream

Mix flour and mustard powder together. Heat butter gently and stir in mixed flour and mustard. Cook for a few seconds, then add warmed milk gradually, stirring all the time. Simmer for about 5 minutes until thick and smooth. Add cream and beat well. Allow sauce to cool. Just before serving, remove any skin that might have formed and beat well again.

If you like a very spicy sauce add more made-up mustard to the finished sauce.

Cumberland Sauce
This is one of the few sweet spiced sauces still to be served with meat in this country. This type of sauce used to be extremely popular. It is especially good with all kinds of roast game, raised pies and any cold meats, particularly ham. It also keeps very well poured into lidded jars or pots, so you can prepare it well in advance of the festive season.

3 oranges	Pinch of salt
3 lemons	1 level dessertspoon dry
1 lb (450 g) good quality	English mustard
redcurrant jelly	1 sherry glass cider vinegar
¼ pt (150 ml) ruby port or sherry	or white wine vinegar
2 tablespoons Grand Marnier	½ teaspoon powdered mace or
(optional)	ground ginger
1 small onion or 4 shallots,	
very finely chopped	

Using a potato peeler, remove rind from all the fruit. Make sure that you remove any pith from rind or this will make your sauce bitter. Shred it as finely as possible—you will not be straining your sauce so the rind must not be in thick chunks.

Put shredded rind into a pan and pour over enough water to cover it. Bring contents to the boil and immediately pour into a strainer. Cool rind under running cold water for a minute or so, and then set aside.

Squeeze and strain juice from 2 oranges and 2 lemons. Bring this to the boil with all remaining ingredients and simmer for 15 minutes over a low heat, stirring all the time to dissolve the redcurrant jelly.

Add shredded rind and boil for a further 5–10 minutes until sauce begins to thicken. Pour into jars or pots and cover. Cool, then refrigerate until sauce is fully thickened. Serve chilled when required.

Spiced Christmas Beef

This is a very old and traditional way of cooking beef dating back to Elizabethan times. In the past, at Christmas the most enormous pieces of meat weighing 40 lb (18 kg) or more would be eaten as part of the 'cold collation' to which guests were treated any time of the day or night over the days of celebration. Spiced beef is not a complicated dish, but it must be planned beforehand as the joint needs to absorb the flavour of the spices for a week. It is delicious and makes a welcome change from turkey and ham on Boxing Day.

5–6 lb (2·5–3 kg) topside or
   brisket of beef
½ teaspoon powdered cloves
½ teaspoon powdered mace
½ teaspoon coarsely crushed
   black pepper
½ teaspoon coarsely crushed
   allspice
1 dessertspoon dried thyme
8 oz (225 g) moist dark brown
   sugar

8 oz (225 g) sea salt
½ oz (15 g) saltpetre
6 fresh or dried bayleaves
12 juniper berries, crushed
1 bouquet garni
2 carrots, chopped
2 sticks celery, chopped
1 onion, chopped
2 wineglasses port
1 pt (500 ml) beef stock

Mix powdered and crushed spices and thyme together. Stir *half* this mixture into sugar. Cover unrolled piece of beef with this spice mixture and put in a shallow earthenware dish. Leave to stand for 24 hours.

Next day, rub salt, saltpetre, bayleaves and crushed juniper berries into meat. Let it steep in this mixture for a week, rubbing it in and turning the meat every day. (You can obtain saltpetre from good chemists or your local butcher, but grocers are no longer able to supply it without a special licence because of the fire risk.)

28

When ready to cook meat, rinse it and soak for 1 hour in cold water. Dry it well, spread reserved spices over inside of beef, roll it up tightly and tie with string. Put joint into a heavy casserole which just fits it. Surround it with bouquet garni and chopped vegetables. Add the 2 glasses of port and stock and cover tightly with a lid. Cook in a low oven 300°F (150°C) Gas Mark 2 for 4–5 hours or until very tender. Allow to cool to lukewarm in cooking liquor, then take meat out and put between two boards with a 1 lb (450 g) weight on top. Leave it like this overnight.

Next day it is ready to eat. Serve sliced, with lots of pickles and plenty of English mustard, and hot baked potatoes.

Yorkshire Christmas Pie (*serves 12*)
Pies have always been extremely popular festive fare, and this particular Christmas pie was famous—and not just in Yorkshire. Originally it was made of a turkey which was stuffed with a goose, which was stuffed with a chicken, which was stuffed with a partridge, which was stuffed with a pigeon! All this was put in a pastry shell, seasoned with mace, nutmeg, cloves and black pepper and surrounded by a jointed hare, and small game birds or wild fowl, covered by a lid of pastry. It must have been an extremely rich dish in its original form. The recipe below has been adapted from an old recipe and is baked in a large pie dish with only a lid of pastry, and with the poultry surrounded by a stuffing mixture.

1 fresh calf's tongue	Salt
1 small goose (5–6 lb) (2·5–3 kg)	Freshly milled black pepper
1 pheasant or chicken	A little butter
(2–2½ lb) (900 g—1·1 kg)	1 lb (450 g) flaky pastry

FOR THE STUFFING:

1 small onion, finely chopped	1 dessertspoon mixed dried
¾ oz (22 g) butter	herbs
1½ lb (675 g) minced pork	1 tablespoon chopped parsley
4 oz (125 g) fresh white	1 egg, beaten
breadcrumbs	A little ground mace or allspice

First, prepare and cook tongue. Soak in cold water for 2–3 hours. Then rinse, put in a pan of cold water, bring to the boil and rinse again. Cook in simmering water until tender, about 1½ hours. Remove from water and peel off skin carefully. Pull out little bones at root and trim away fat if necessary.

Bone out goose and chicken (or pheasant)–you may be able to persuade your butcher to do this. Reserve bones for stock. Season inside of each bird, then place tongue inside the chicken (or pheasant) and place this inside goose. Rub goose with a little butter, and season; roll up.

To prepare stuffing, soften onion in butter, then mix with minced pork, breadcrumbs and herbs. Bind with egg and season well, adding a little ground mace or allspice.

Pre-set oven at 400°F (200°C) Gas Mark 6.

Line bottom and sides of 15–16in (38·5–40cm) diameter pie dish with stuffing, keeping back a little for top. Put rolled-up goose in centre and cover with a thin layer of remaining stuffing. Roll out pastry and cover pie, making a small hole in centre. Trim and decorate as you like. Brush with egg wash (beaten egg mixed with cold water and a little salt). Place pie in centre of pre-heated oven and bake for 40–50 minutes or until brown. Then cover pie with a double sheet of wet greaseproof paper, lower heat to 360°F (180°C) Gas Mark 4 and continue to cook for a further 1½–2 hours.

Meanwhile, make a stock from the poultry bones, with some root vegetables and herbs to flavour.

Remove pie from oven when cooked and leave to cool. Leave stock to cool in refrigerator.

When pie is completely cold, fill up with jellied stock through hole in centre of pie. Serve cold, cut into wedges accompanied by plenty of pickles. Spiced Orange Rings (page 24), Pickled Pears (page 25), and Spiced Prunes (page 25) are delicious with this dish.

Brandy-Soaked Oranges and Almond Cream (*serves 6*)
This is a very old recipe and quite delicious. Try serving this very refreshing sweet as an alternative to Christmas pud!

3 or 4 large oranges	1½ tablespoons caster sugar
2–3 tablespoons brandy	1 oz (25 g) ground almonds
½ pt (250 ml) double cream	Toasted flaked almonds for
Finely grated rind and juice of	decoration
1 lemon	

Peel the oranges and divide carefully into segments. Marinate in the brandy for at least 1 hour. Whip the cream until stiff, beat in the lemon juice, grated rind and ground almonds. Lastly beat in the sugar. Whip well once more and then chill in the refrigerator. When you are ready to serve the sweet, place the orange segments and brandy in your prettiest glasses and top with the almond cream. Decorate with toasted flaked almonds or tinsel bows, artificial or real flowers, baubles or anything you can think up. Make them as pretty as possible because Christmas is special.

Champagne Sorbet (*serves 6*)
In the nineteenth century it was common to serve at least ten courses at a great Christmas feast. To refresh the palate and aid digestion, sorbets were served half-way through the meal (a survival of the

sweetmeat that rounded off the courses in medieval times). They are lighter and more refreshing than ice creams. These sorbets were often flavoured with port, brandy, rum or wine and here is one such recipe. You can use a sparkling white wine rather than champagne if you want, but Christmas only comes once a year!

10 oz (275 g) sugar	3 tablespoons lemon juice
8 fl oz (180 ml) water	2 egg whites
1 pt (500 ml) sparkling white wine or champagne	4 tablespoons icing sugar

Dissolve sugar in water over low heat, then bring to boil, and continue boiling for 5 minutes until thick, but not brown. Cool, then stir in 12 fl oz (330 ml) wine or champagne and the lemon juice. Pour into freezer trays or container and freeze for 1 hour. Then pour mixture into a basin and beat well for 2 minutes. Freeze for a further 30 minutes. Beat again. Repeat freezing and beating every 30 minutes for the next 2 hours.

Whisk egg whites until stiff and gradually beat in icing sugar. Beat frozen mixture again to break down ice-crystals. Fold in egg white and sugar mixture. Freeze again until firm.

Half an hour before you want to serve your sorbet, remove it from freezer and put in refrigerator to soften slightly. Meanwhile, dip edges of six stemmed wine glasses into water and then into caster sugar coloured pale yellow or green with food colouring. (This will give beautiful frosted edges to your glasses.) Fill with scoops of sorbet and pour a little of the remaining wine, or champagne, over each portion. Decorate with sprigs of mint and serve immediately.

It is best to serve this refreshing sorbet after the main course, and before the Christmas pudding and other rich goodies arrive!

Everlasting Syllabub (*serves 6–8*)

From Tudor and Stuart times, entertaining at Christmas required the mistress of the manor to be an expert in preparing syllabub. Every house had its particular favourite, but basically it was a confection of white wine and spirits, or cider and ale, well sweetened with sugar and flavoured with lemon, nutmeg or rosemary to which cream or milk was added.

Originally served in a punch bowl, syllabub was more a drink than a whip. It gradually became thicker and was spooned out of a glass rather than drunk, but the creamy whip still separated from the clear alcoholic liquid. In Georgian times, it was discovered that by reducing the proportions of wine and sugar to cream, the whip would remain thick and light without separating. This version was called a 'solid' or 'everlasting' syllabub. The recipe given here is of this type and one which I have found very successful.

4 tablespoons white wine or	A little freshly grated nutmeg
sherry	4 oz (125 g) caster sugar
4 tablespoons brandy	Sprig of rosemary
2 lemons	1 pt (500 ml) double cream

The day before the syllabub is to be made, put thinly pared rind and juice of lemons in a bowl with the wine, brandy, nutmeg, sugar and rosemary. Stir until the sugar is dissolved, and leave to stand overnight.

Next day, strain mixture into a large deep bowl. Pour in the cream slowly, stirring all the time. Whisk mixture with a rotary or balloon whisk until it thickens and will hold a soft peak on the whisk. (This process may take 5 minutes or as long as 15 minutes depending on thickness of cream, temperature and method of whisking.) Avoid using an electric hand whisk if you can, because a few seconds too long and the cream will be a grainy mass and unusable.

When cream is ready, spoon into wine glasses. Decorate with a tiny sprig of rosemary, or a twist of lemon peel or a small piece of crystallised fruit and a sprinkling of grated nutmeg. Keep in a cool place—preferably not the refrigerator—until you are ready to serve. It can be made at least 2 days before needed, and will not spoil or separate, once in the glasses.

Serve with Almond Shortbread (page 60), Langue de Chat Biscuits (page 94), or Mothering Sunday Wafers (page 73).

Variations:

Ginger Syllabub

Use basic recipe, adding 2 large pinches ginger instead of lemon rind, and 4 pieces stem ginger finely chopped and added to finished syllabub. Serve with homemade brandy snaps.

Fruit Syllabub

Use basic recipe and fold any fruit purée into finished syllabub. Soft fruits such as raspberries, strawberries and redcurrants are most successful, but do experiment.

Brandy Ice Cream (serves 6–8)

Ice cream began to be made in the eighteenth century as a result of the development of ice-houses on country estates. Finely sieved fruits were worked with sugar and scalded cream and frozen. Pewterers produced sets of basins to make ice cream; an inner smaller one to contain the cream and fruit and an outer larger one to hold the ice all around it.

This ice cream is even more delicious served with a mincemeat sauce. Stir a little extra brandy into some homemade mincemeat and heat gently. Pour over the Brandy Ice Cream just before serving.

| 4 eggs, separated | 3 tablespoons brandy |
| 4 oz (125 g) caster sugar | ¾ pt (400 ml) double cream |

Beat egg yolks with sugar and brandy. Whip double cream and add to mixture. Whisk egg whites until stiff and fold into cream mixture. Freeze in a lidded container.

Remove from freezer 30 minutes before serving and leave in refrigerator for flavour to emerge. Scoop into bowls and serve with mincemeat sauce, if you wish, and Langue de Chat Biscuits (see recipe on page 94).

Chestnut Ice Cream with Chocolate Sauce (*serves 6*)

4 eggs, separated	4 oz (125 g) plain } for
4 oz (125 g) caster sugar	chocolate } chocolate
1 tablespoon rum or kirsch	3 tablespoons milk } sauce
¾ pt (400 ml) double cream	Whipped cream and
1 lb (450 g) tin of unsweetened chestnut purée	crystallised chestnuts

Beat egg yolks with sugar and rum. Whip double cream until it stands in peaks and add to egg yolk mixture. Stir in chestnut purée. Whisk egg whites until stiff and add to mixture. Freeze in a polythene container.

To make sauce, melt chocolate in a basin over hot water together with the milk. Leave this thick sauce to cool.

Take ice cream out of freezer 30 minutes before you want to serve it, and leave in refrigerator to improve flavour. Scoop ice cream into pretty stemmed glasses and top with cold chocolate sauce. Decorate with a little whipped cream and a few crystallised chestnuts (see recipe on page 46).

For a special Christmas meal serve scoops of Chestnut Ice Cream in a meringue basket.

Christmas Ice Cream (*serves 6–8*)
You can experiment with this recipe if you want, by adding different nuts and crystallised fruits—see what delicious combinations you can invent!

4 eggs, separated	2 tablespoons brandy or rum
4 oz (125 g) caster sugar	2 oz (50 g) hazelnuts, roasted
¾ pt (400 ml) double cream	and chopped
2 teaspoons coffee essence	4 oz (125 g) dates, chopped
4 oz (125 g) brown breadcrumbs	4 oz (125 g) glacé cherries, quartered
1 teaspoon mixed spice	2 oz (50 g) candied peel,
6 oz (175 g) raisins	chopped

Beat egg yolks with sugar. Whip cream and add to egg yolk mixture with coffee essence, breadcrumbs and spice. Whip egg whites until stiff and add to mixture. Pour into a plastic container with a lid and freeze until half-set.

Meanwhile, soak raisins in brandy or rum for at least one hour. Prepare other chosen ingredients, and gently mix these with raisins and brandy into semi-set ice cream. Freeze until firm. Remove from the freezer 20 minutes before serving and put in the refrigerator.

To serve, scoop out ice cream and pile into your prettiest glass or china dish. Decorate with holly, Christmas baubles, and red ribbon. Alternatively this ice cream can be frozen in a basin, turned out on to a plate to look like a Christmas pudding and decorated with holly.

Ginger Ice Cream (*serves 6–8*)

4 eggs, separated
4 oz (125 g) caster sugar
1 teaspoon ground ginger

2 tablespoons brandy
$\frac{3}{4}$ pt (400 ml) double cream
4 large pieces stem ginger

Beat egg yolks with sugar, ground ginger, and brandy. Whip cream and add to egg yolk mixture. Whip egg whites stiffly and fold into mixture. Pour into a lidded container and freeze until almost set. Add chopped stem ginger and mix evenly into semi-set ice cream. Return to freezer until completely set.

Remove from freezer 20 minutes before serving and put in refrigerator. Scoop out and serve piled in stemmed glasses with extra slices of stem ginger and crushed brandy snaps to decorate.

Rich Coffee and Praline Ice Cream (*serves 6–8*)·

FOR PRALINE:
3 oz (75 g) unblanched almonds   3 oz (75 g) granulated sugar

FOR ICE CREAM:
4 eggs, separated
4 oz (125 g) caster sugar

3 tablespoons coffee essence
$\frac{3}{4}$ pt (400 ml) double cream

To make praline, place unblanched almonds and the granulated sugar in a small, preferably non-stick, frying pan. Heat gently until sugar melts. Stir with a metal spoon until a rich dark brown. Turn out on to an oiled baking tray and leave to set.

To make ice cream, beat egg yolks with caster sugar and coffee essence. Whip cream and add to egg yolk mixture. Whip egg whites until stiff and gently stir into egg and cream mixture.

Crush set praline into a coarse powder with a rolling pin or in a nut mill or a mincer. Stir this into ice-cream mixture. Freeze in ice-trays or any container until half-set; then stir to distribute praline evenly. Return to the freezer until firm.

Remove from the freezer 20 minutes before you want to serve and put in refrigerator. Serve piled in scoops in a Brandy and Ginger Snap Basket (see following recipe). Decorate with a sprinkling of extra praline powder if you want.

Brandy and Ginger Snap Basket

1½ oz (40 g) softened butter
1½ oz (40 g) golden syrup
1½ oz (40 g) caster sugar

1½ oz (40 g) plain flour
½ level teaspoon ground ginger
1 teaspoon brandy

Pre-set oven at 350°F (180°C) Gas Mark 4.

Place all ingredients in a blender and blend until thoroughly mixed together.

Line a baking tray with non-stick bakewell paper, and spread on mixture into a round about ¼in (5cm) thick, using a small palette knife. Allow plenty of room for mixture to spread during cooking.

Bake in pre-heated oven for 15–20 minutes until bubbling and golden brown. Remove from oven and leave to stand for a few seconds to firm up. Have ready a 2 pt (1·25 l) round casserole turned upside down. Oil its outer surface well. Also have another sheet of non-stick paper handy.

When the brandy and ginger round has firmed up slightly, flip it on to your second sheet of paper. Immediately, lift it with the help of the paper on to your upturned casserole dish, pressing lightly to form a fluted edge. Peel off the paper and leave to set on casserole. When firm, lift basket off casserole and store in an airtight tin until ready to fill with ice cream. Make sure you keep the basket in a dry atmosphere and try not to cook it earlier than the day before you need it.

Old English Port Wine Jelly (*serves 6–8*)

Jelly has been an established feasting dish since medieval days, originally in a savoury form. In Tudor and Stuart times it was sweetened and served as a final course at the banquet. Wine jellies were extremely popular and have remained so. This recipe is strictly for grown-ups!

3–4 oz (75 g–125 g) granulated
  sugar
½ pt (250 ml) water
1 in (2·5 cm) piece cinnamon
  stick
3 cloves
1 blade mace

Finely grated rind and juice of
  1 lemon
1 oz (25 g) powdered gelatine
½ pt (250 ml) good quality ruby
  port
Black grapes for decoration

Place 3 oz (75 g) sugar in a saucepan with water and cinnamon stick, cloves, mace and lemon rind. Cover and bring to boil, then remove from heat and leave to infuse for about 15 minutes.

Meanwhile, place 4 tablespoons cold water in a small basin and stir in powdered gelatine. (If you wish to serve your wine jelly in a bowl, 1 oz (25 g) gelatine will be sufficient, but if you wish to turn it out of a mould, I should add an extra teaspoonful. Do check quantities on the packet, because different makes can vary in strength.) Leave for 5 minutes to absorb water, then sit basin in a saucepan of hot water and leave until gelatine melts and liquid becomes completely clear.

Strain spices and lemon rind from sugar syrup and pass liquid gelatine and lemon juice through the sieve. Stir port into resulting clear liquid. (You must use a decent port or the jelly will not be worth eating.) Taste, and add extra sugar if necessary. Don't worry if you think the flavour is rather strong at this point—it won't be once the jelly is chilled.

Pour liquid jelly into an old-fashioned bowl or 8 stemmed glasses. If you have a pretty mould, use this. (You can still find lovely Victorian moulds in junk shops very cheaply, and one of these would be ideal for this recipe.)

Leave your jelly to set in a cool place. Serve slightly chilled and decorated with bunches of black grapes that have been dipped in lightly beaten white of an egg, then in caster sugar and left to dry overnight on greaseproof paper.

Plum Pudding with Lemon Syrup

This recipe uses butter or margarine instead of suet, so the pudding is lighter and more suitable for young children and elderly people. It can also be made as late as Christmas Eve. Lemon syrup is poured over the pudding just before serving, instead of rum or brandy.

4 oz (125 g) plain flour
Pinch of salt
1 teaspoon mixed spice
$\frac{1}{2}$ teaspoon ground cinnamon
$\frac{1}{4}$ teaspoon ground nutmeg
4 oz (125 g) fresh white
  breadcrumbs
4 oz (125 g) soft brown sugar
4 oz (125 g) butter or
  margarine

6 oz (175 g) sultanas
8 oz (225g) seedless raisins
2 oz (50 g) candied peel
1 dessert apple
2 oz (50 g) prunes
2 oz (50g) golden syrup
Finely grated rind and juice
  of 1 lemon
2 eggs, beaten
$2\frac{1}{2}$ fl oz (65 ml) brandy

FOR THE SYRUP:
3 oz (75 g) caster sugar
Juice of 1 large lemon

$\frac{1}{4}$ pt (150 ml) water
2 tablespoons Cointreau

36

Sieve flour, salt and spices together into a large bowl. Mix in breadcrumbs and sugar. Rub in butter or margarine. Add sultanas, raisins and candied peel. Peel apple and grate into mixture. Chop prunes, add to mixture and stir well.

Warm the golden syrup and stir into the mixture. Add lemon rind and juice, beaten eggs and brandy. Mix thoroughly. Turn into a greased 2–2½ pt (1–1·3 l) pudding basin (or 2 greased 1 pt (500 ml) basins) and level the surface. Cover with a piece of buttered paper and a square of white cotton cloth or muslin, or aluminium foil 12in (30cm) larger than the width of your pudding basin. Make a pleat across centre of pudding cloth. Tie down securely with string and open pleat to leave room for the pudding to rise.

Place the pudding in the top of a steamer, double boiler, or in a large pan of gently boiling water. Steam for 6 hours (until a rich dark colour if using a glass basin) topping up the water level from time to time. Make sure the pudding does not go off the boil and always top up with *boiling* water.

When pudding is cooked, lift out and remove covering to prevent condensation from the steam. When cold, re-cover with buttered greaseproof paper. Wrap in foil, seal carefully and store in a dry, cool place.

To reheat for Christmas lunch steam your pudding again for 1½–2 hours.

To make the lemon syrup, put sugar, lemon juice and water in a small pan. Heat gently to dissolve sugar, and then bring to boil. Boil rapidly for 3 minutes. Add Cointreau and stir.

To serve, uncover pudding, spear several times with a skewer and pour on syrup. Turn out carefully on to a hot plate. Dust with sifted icing sugar and decorate with a sprig of holly. (Remember to cover the stem of the holly with cling film, because it shouldn't come into contact with the pudding.) Serve with chilled whipped cream, flavoured with a few drops of vanilla essence and sweetened with a little caster sugar.

Preserved Peaches (*serves 6*)
These make a lovely dessert to enjoy at Christmas or any other time. They also make a super present for a special person. If you preserve the peaches in August when they are at their best and reasonably priced you won't find this recipe too expensive.

6 medium peaches	2 in (5 cm) piece of cinnamon
Juice from 1 lemon	stick
6 cloves	¼ teaspoon ground mace
¾ pt (400 ml) water	¼ pt (150 ml) brandy
12 oz (350 g) sugar	

Cover peaches with boiling water for 2 minutes. Remove from water and skin. Brush lemon juice all over peaches to stop them going brown. Stick a clove in each one. Combine water, sugar, cinnamon and mace in a saucepan; bring to boil and cook until sugar has dissolved. Add the peaches and cook for 5–10 minutes or until tender. Place peaches in a wide-necked jar; stir brandy into syrup and pour over fruit. Leave to cool.

Cover tightly and leave to stand in a cool place until needed, or for at least 3 days—if you can bear to wait that long!

Rich Old English Sherry Trifle (*serves* 8)

The trifle dates back to Elizabethan days and has always been part of English festive fare. An Elizabethan trifle was made like this: 'Take a pint of thick cream and season it with sugar, ginger and rosewater, so stir it as you would then have it, and make it lukewarm in a chafing dish on coals, and after, put it into a silver bowl and so serve it.'

In later recipes the cream was boiled and lightly renneted to make it thicker and 'when you serve it, strew on some French comfits', which were sugar-coated coriander or caraway seeds—our modern 'hundreds and thousands'? By 1751 trifle was being made with broken Naples biscuits (sponge biscuits), macaroons and ratafia cakes melted with 'sack at the bottom of the bowl, good boiled custard in the middle and put a syllabub over that'. Subsequent recipes replaced the syllabub topping with whipped cream and the modern trifle was established. Sometimes I put a syllabub topping on trifle instead of cream—it is absolutely delicious and very rich.

FOR BASE:
2 x 7 in (18 cm) fatless sponge cakes or 1 packet sponge cakes
1 lb (450 g) apricot jam, apple or quince jelly
4 oz (125 g) ratafias or macaroons
¼ bottle medium dry sherry or Madeira

FOR CUSTARD:
1 pt (500 ml) milk
Vanilla pod, pierced
2 oz (50 g) caster sugar
2 teaspoons cornflour
5 eggs
1 pt (500 ml) double cream

FOR DECORATION:
4 oz (115 g) glace cherries
4 oz (125 g) blanched almonds
2 oz (50 g) crystallised apricots
2 oz (50 g) crystallised chestnuts
2 oz (50 g) crystallised pineapple
4 oz (125 g) ratafia biscuits
Crystallised angelica leaves

Split sponge cakes or sponge bases in half, and liberally spread with chosen preserve. Sandwich together and cut into 1in (2·5cm) fingers. Arrange in your prettiest shallow dish—you will need one about 12in (30cm) across top and 3in (7·5)cm deep. Sprinkle with ratafias or macaroons and plenty of sherry or Madeira and set aside.

To make custard, bring milk with vanilla pod to the boil. Mix sugar with cornflour, add eggs gradually and beat well until smooth. Remove vanilla pod from milk and pour on to egg mixture stirring all the time. Rinse out milk pan, leaving a film of cold water in bottom. Return custard to pan and stir well with a wooden spoon over a low heat until thick. Plunge bottom of pan, immediately custard is thick enough, into a bowl of cold water to stop mixture curdling. Leave to cool a little.

When custard is fairly cool, pour over the sponge, and leave to cool completely. When cool, whip cream until it stands in peaks and spread a thick layer over custard. Pipe top with remaining cream and decorate with loads of crystallised fruits and nuts and ratafias —the more the merrier!

If you want to put on a syllabub topping instead of cream, see the recipe for Everlasting Syllabub (page 31). To serve at other times of the year, this trifle can be decorated with crystallised flowers— a full-blown crystallised rose or just rose-petals look beautiful.

Rum and Chestnut Creams (*serves 6*)

Years ago chestnuts were used in cooking much more than they are now, and these creams are based on a very old recipe. They are very rich and would make an unusual alternative to Christmas pudding on the great day.

1 lb (450 g) fresh chestnuts
  (or tin of unsweetened
  chestnut pureé)
½ pt (250 ml) milk
Vanilla pod

½ pt (250 ml) double cream
Juice and rind of 1 orange
2 sherry glasses Jamaican rum
2 oz (50 g) caster sugar

To make your own purée, peel and skin chestnuts and poach in the milk with a piece of vanilla pod, until tender. Put through a sieve and cool before using.

Dissolve caster sugar in rum over a low heat and allow to cool. Beat in chestnut purée. Whip cream together with orange rind and juice. Fold into rum-flavoured purée. Taste and add extra caster sugar if necessary. Pipe chestnut cream into goblets and chill well. Just before serving, decorate with lightly sweetened, rum-flavoured whipped cream and a segment of crystallised orange, or coat surface of each cream with clear honey and sprinkle with Demerara sugar.

Serve with sponge finger biscuits.

Traditional Plum Pudding (*makes 5 x 1 lb (450 g) puddings*)
Plum Pudding did not become associated with Christmas fare until the nineteenth century when Prince Albert introduced it, because he was so fond of this heavy rich pudding.

Plum porridge or pottage was the earliest form of plum pudding and dates back to medieval times. This was made from meat, usually shin of beef and veal, stewed together with currants, raisins, prunes (the dried plums which give their name to the mixture), spices, sugar, sack (a once popular wine from the Canary Islands), lemon juice and claret. The whole thing was thickened with brown breadcrumbs or sago. By the nineteenth century, meat had been left out and the pudding became more like our modern-day Christmas pudding.

The idea of putting silver trinkets and charms into the pudding probably came from the earlier tradition of the beans inside the Twelfth Night Cake, but this has since died out. It is still traditional to bury a silver coin, if you have one, in the mixture. All the family should stir the pudding in turn on 'Stir Up Sunday', the Sunday before Advent, and make a wish at the same time. The coin should then be pushed in, plus a ring and a thimble; the coin is to bring wordly fortune, the ring a marriage and the thimble a life of blessedness.

8 oz (225 g) large prunes
8 oz (225 g) currants
8 oz (225 g) sultanas
8 oz (225 g) large raisins
8 oz (225 g) self-raising flour
¼ teaspoon salt
½ teaspoon baking powder
1 teaspoon mixed spice
½ teaspoon grated nutmeg
½ teaspoon cinnamon
½ teaspoon ground ginger
1 lb (450 g) fresh white
   breadcrumbs
8 oz (225g) soft dark brown
   sugar
8 oz (225 g) shredded butcher's
   beef suet

2 oz (50 g) candied citron peel,
   chopped
2 oz (50 g) candied orange and
   lemon peel, finely chopped
4 oz (125 g) blanched almonds,
   chopped
4 oz (125 g) carrots, grated
4 oz (125 g) cooking apple,
   grated
Grated rind and juice of 1
   orange
Grated rind and juice of 1
   lemon
½ pt (250 ml) stout
3 eggs, beaten
Rum to mix, about 4
   tablespoons

Soak prunes overnight in cold tea. Next day, drain, remove stones and chop finely. The addition of prunes gives a richer, darker colour to the pudding as well as a very good flavour. Wash and dry all remaining dried fruit and stone raisins if necessary.

Sieve flour, baking powder and spices together into a very

large bowl. Add breadcrumbs, sugar and suet, mixing in each ingredient thoroughly. Gradually mix in all the dried fruit, candied peel and nuts. Stir in the rind and juice of the lemon and orange, followed by grated carrot and apple. Pour in the stout and mix until smooth. Cover basin with a clean cloth and leave in a cool place overnight or longer if convenient (the flavour will be improved). In fact, the mixture can be left to stand for a fortnight or longer at this point. Stir mixture every day if you decide to do this.

On the day you want to cook the puddings, add the beaten eggs. Stir furiously until the pudding ingredients are thoroughly blended. Add enough rum to make a soft dropping consistency. Spoon mixture into greased pudding basins to come within 1in (2·5cm) of rim, packing mixture down well with the back of a wooden spoon. You will need 5 x 1 lb (450 g) basins or 2 x 2 lb (900 g) and 1 x 1 lb (450 g) basins. Cover top of each with greased greaseproof paper. Put a thick layer of flour on top of the greaseproof, pressing it down well. (This will become a solid paste and act as a seal both for cooking and storing.) Then cover with another piece of greaseproof paper. Finally, cover basins with a pudding cloth, muslin or aluminium foil, making a pleat in centre to allow room for puddings to rise during cooking. Tie securely with string and make a handle of string across the top of each basin, so that you can lift the puddings in and out of the pan easily.

Place puddings in a steamer, double boiler, or in a large pan of gently boiling water. Steam for at least 6 hours topping up water level from time to time with *boiling* water. When cooked, remove puddings from pan and leave until cold. Renew top piece of greaseproof and cloth and store in a cool dry place until needed.

On the great day, steam again for 2–3 hours before serving. Turn out on to a large platter. Sprinkle with icing sugar. Heat some brandy, whisky, rum or kirsch in a small saucepan or ladle. Pour over pudding and set alight. Bring pudding to table burning and surrounded by a hedge of holly. Any spirit can be used, but you will find that rum burns for longer. Make sure your holly doesn't go up in smoke!

Brandy and Lemon Butter (*serves 6*)
This hard sauce can be made two or three weeks before Christmas and kept in the refrigerator until needed. This will help the busy cook.

4 oz (125 g) unsalted butter	1 tablespoon boiling water
4 oz (125 g) caster sugar	1 teaspoon lemon juice
½ teaspoon lemon rind, grated	4 tablespoons brandy

Cut butter into small pieces and put with sugar and lemon rind in a warmed bowl. Beat until creamy, add boiling water and continue to beat until every grain of sugar has dissolved. This will stop the butter tasting gritty. Add lemon juice and brandy *a little at a time*, beating thoroughly. This will prevent curdling. When completely blended, press into lidded wax cartons or jars and store in refrigerator until needed. Serve cold, sprinkled with grated lemon rind, to accompany Christmas pudding, or put a large spoonful under the lid of each hot mince pie just before serving.

Try adding pieces of chopped glacé cherries—you can buy green and yellow as well as red—and chopped angelica. Your brandy butter will look very colourful and taste even more mouth-watering.

Rum and Orange Butter (*serves 4–6*)
This alternative to Brandy and Lemon Butter can also be made two or three weeks before Christmas and stored in the refrigerator, and either can be frozen if desired.

4 oz (125 g) unsalted butter	1 teaspoon orange juice
4 oz (125 g) soft brown sugar	4 tablespoons dark rum
½ teaspoon orange rind, grated	Extra orange rind for decoration
1 tablespoon boiling water	

The method is exactly the same as for Brandy and Lemon Butter substituting orange rind and juice for lemon and rum for brandy. Serve chilled and sprinkled with grated orange rind.

Traditional Cumberland Rum Butter (*serves 8*)
Originally, this hard sauce was spread on biscuits and served with mulled ale or wine to guests who came to welcome a new baby. The baby was often given a spoonful too—the butter was said to promise the goodness of life; the rum, the spirit of life; the sugar, the sweetness of life; and the nutmeg, the spice of life. Nowadays it is served with Christmas pudding and mince pies and may be made several weeks before needed and stored in the refrigerator. Traditionally rum butter was put in beautiful old china dishes with lids and I can remember one such dish which has been passed from generation to generation in our family. Its delicious smell of rum always means Christmas to me. However the butter can be stored in any suitable dish, or in several smaller pots or jars until needed. Try serving it at other times of the year, with a rich steamed pudding, such as Spiced Fig Pudding (see recipe on page 74).

8 oz (225 g) unsalted butter	Pinch of ground cinnamon
12 oz (350 g) soft brown sugar	Pinch of freshly grated nutmeg
6 fl oz (175 ml) rum	

Put the butter in an ovenproof bowl and place in a very low oven until it melts. Stir in the sugar and let it dissolve completely. Pour in the rum a little at a time, beating the mixture continuously. Flavour with the spices. Pour into a dish or several small pots and leave to harden. Serve in slices on top of steaming hot Christmas pudding.

Georgian Fairy Butter (*serves 6–8*)

The Georgians served this on its own as a sweet, but we would find it too rich. It is, however, delicious served with Christmas pudding or mince pies instead of brandy butter. Use it at other times of the year as a cake filling or to decorate cold puddings. It is very good as a filling for meringues and small choux buns.

4 oz (125 g) unsalted butter
2 oz (50g) caster sugar
3 hard-boiled egg yolks
1 teaspoon very finely grated
   orange rind

1 tablespoon orange-flower
   water, brandy, rum or
   lemon juice

Cream butter and sugar together. Mash egg yolks and beat into creamed mixture with chosen flavouring. Pass through a sieve, preferably a hair sieve, and carefully pile into a pretty shallow serving dish, using two forks. This way you will not destroy the 'fairy' texture. Scatter finely grated orange rind over your Fairy Butter and serve.

This butter can be made 2 or 3 days before you need it and kept in a cool place.

Fluffy Brandy Sauce (*serves 6*)

This can be served as an alternative to brandy or rum butter. It is lighter in texture, not so rich, and very good with any rich fruit pudding. It can be made in advance and kept in the refrigerator until needed.

1 egg, separated
4 oz (125 g) icing sugar, sieved
3 tablespoons brandy

¼ pt (150 ml) double cream,
   whipped

Beat egg white until foamy. Add 2 oz (50 g) icing sugar, a little at a time, beating well after each addition until mixture is stiff enough to stand in peaks. In a second basin, beat egg yolk and remaining 2 oz (50 g) icing sugar until mixture thickens. Fold into egg white and sugar mixture together with whipped cream and brandy.

Serve in your prettiest bowl. (This is also very good with hot mince pies.)

Traditional Rum Sauce *(serves 6–8)*

Many people prefer this hot rum-flavoured white sauce with Christmas Pudding, rather than Brandy or Rum Butter. Try it and see what you think.

1½ oz (40 g) butter
¾ pt (400 ml) milk
2 level tablespoons plain flour

1½ tablespoons caster sugar
2-3 tablespoons rum

Melt butter slowly in a saucepan. Warm milk in another pan. Add flour to butter and, stirring continuously, cook over a gentle heat for a few minutes. Remove from heat and add warmed milk a little at a time stirring until smooth. Stir in sugar when all milk has been added, and mixture is creamy and smooth. Continue to cook sauce gently for 5 minutes stirring all the time. Then add rum and taste. Add more sugar if needed.

Serve in your prettiest sauce-boat with the Christmas Pudding or any other rich fruit pudding.

Rich Rum Sauce with Sweet White Wine *(serves 6–8)*

This is a very old recipe for Rum Sauce. It is extremely rich, and when served with a rich Christmas pudding is unforgettable.

5 egg yolks
2 oz (50 g) caster sugar
Rind of 1 lemon

½ pt (250 ml) Sauterne (or
  other sweet white wine)
3 tablespoons Jamaican rum

Cream egg yolks and sugar in a basin until sugar has dissolved. Remove rind from lemon with a potato peeler and shred very, very finely. Add to egg yolk and sugar mixture and stir in wine and rum.

Set the basin over a saucepan of boiling water making sure the water is in contact with the bottom of the basin. Whisk sauce slowly but continuously with a balloon whisk until it is as thick as double cream. Remove from heat and continue whisking until sauce has cooled a little. Keep sauce warm over a pan of hot, but not boiling water. This time the water must *not* be in contact with bottom of basin. Serve warm with Christmas pudding.

Valencia Sauce *(serves 6–8)*

This delicious and refreshing sauce can be served with Christmas pudding instead of Rum Sauce. It is based on an old recipe, and clementines or tangerines can be used instead of the orange.

1 large orange
1½ oz (40g) butter
1½ oz (40 g) plain flour
1 pt (500 ml) milk

2 level tablespoons demerara
  sugar
1 miniature bottle Grand
  Marnier or Cointreau

44

Finely grate rind from orange and reserve. Remove all pith from orange and cut into segments. Cut each segment in half. Melt butter in a medium-sized saucepan and stir in flour. Cook gently for a few minutes, and then remove from heat and add milk slowly a little at a time, stirring continuously. Return to heat and bring slowly to the boil stirring all the time. Add orange rind, sugar, liqueur and orange segments. Stir gently over heat for 2–3 minutes.

Serve hot with Christmas pudding or mince pies.

Wine and Brandy Sauce (*serves 6*)

This delicate pink wine sauce is lighter than traditional rum sauce. It can be made early on Christmas morning and reheated when required. Sweet sherry may be used instead of the red wine if you prefer.

2 egg yolks	8 fl oz (220 ml) port-type wine
2 oz (50 g) caster sugar	2 tablespoons brandy or
2 level teaspoons cornflour	orange-flavoured liqueur

Put egg yolks and sugar in a basin. Whisk together until sugar has dissolved and mixture is light in colour. This is best done with a balloon or rotary whisk. Beat in remaining ingredients, dissolving cornflour in a little of the wine. Stand basin over a pan of boiling water and whisk with a balloon whisk until thickened.

Reheat when required and serve with Christmas pudding.

Chocolate Rum Truffles (*makes about 12 oz (350 g)*)

Traditionally, these mouthwatering sweets have been associated with Christmas, but are delicious as an after-dinner sweet at any time. This particular recipe contains fresh cream, so they should be eaten up quickly! Some people don't like the flavour of rum, so replace it with brandy, or Grand Marnier or any favourite liqueur.

6 oz (175 g) plain chocolate	1 oz (25 g) butter
6 oz (175 g) milk chocolate	1 tablespoon rum
2 egg yolks	1 dessertspoon double cream

Melt the chocolate in a bowl over hot water, then add the egg yolks, butter, rum and cream. Stir until the mixture is thick enough to handle. Cool slightly, then form into balls and roll in grated chocolate or chocolate powder. Leave overnight until firm. The next day put in paper cases or in a dish covered with a gold doily and eat them!

(I would suggest you use a good quality dessert chocolate and *not* cooking chocolate for this recipe.)

Christmas Fudge *(makes about 2½ lb (1·1 kg))*

Homemade sweets make lovely Christmas presents. This is a smooth creamy fudge full of nuts and fruit. Try out your own variations using any nuts, and dried or glacé fruits.

½ pt (250 ml) milk
1¾ lb (800 g) granulated sugar
4 oz (125 g) butter
2 teaspoons vanilla essence
½ oz (15 g) currants or sultanas
½ oz (15 g) walnuts, chopped
½ oz (15 g) glacé cherries, chopped
½ oz (15 g) blanched almonds, chopped
½ oz (15 g) candied angelica, chopped

Grease a 7in (18cm) square tin. Pour milk into a heavy-based saucepan and bring slowly to boil. Add sugar and butter and heat slowly, stirring all the time, until sugar dissolves and butter melts.

Bring mixture to boil, cover pan and boil for 2 minutes. Uncover and continue to boil steadily to 240°F (116°C) or soft ball stage, stirring occasionally. (To test without a thermometer, place small drop of syrup into cold water. If rolled with the fingers syrup should form a soft ball.)

Remove pan from heat. Stir in vanilla essence, fruit, nuts, and angelica and leave to cool for 5 minutes. Beat fudge until it just begins to lose its gloss and is thick and creamy. Pour it into prepared tin. Mark it into squares when cool and cut with a sharp knife when set.

Crystallised Chestnuts *(makes 1½ lb (675 g))*

These have been made and eaten at Christmas-time in this country for centuries, but now those you can buy from the shops seem to come from France and are very expensive. Try making your own.

1 lb (450 g) large fresh chestnuts
1 lb (450 g) granulated sugar
¼ pt (150 ml) water
½ teaspoon vanilla essence

Gently slit the skins of the chestnuts with a sharp knife, but be careful not to cut into the nuts. Boil the nuts for 20 minutes, then skin them while still warm. Make a syrup from the sugar and water, stirring to dissolve the sugar and boiling them together. Add the vanilla essence and the chestnuts. Boil briskly for 10 minutes, then take the nuts out and drain them on a wire rack.

Leave for 24 hours and then re-boil the syrup, put the nuts back and simmer until they are thickly coated. Drain as before, and allow to dry before putting into airtight containers. Packed into pretty boxes, they make delightful presents.

Crystallised Fruits

Crystallised or candied fruits have been very popular at special banquets since Tudor times. They were eaten at the end of the meal and also offered as refreshment to callers at other times of the day. The variety of plants and fruits that have been candied over the years is enormous—angelica, stalks of lettuce, green walnuts, apricots, peaches, damsons, plums, oranges, lemons, parsley and fennel roots, pear, borage, even sea-holly, to name but a few!

Nowadays, we eat crystallised fruits at Christmas only, and they are very expensive, but so delicious, Try making your own; it is most rewarding and much cheaper. Don't be put off because the process seems to be complicated—it isn't!

2 lb (900 g) fresh fruit—a mixture of, say, oranges, satsumas, tangerines, seedless grapes or any other fruit you like.

BASIC SUGAR SYRUP:

12 oz (350 g) granulated sugar   1 pt (500 ml) water

FOR RE-BOILING:

14 oz (400 g) granulated sugar

Remove peel and pith from oranges, or whatever fruit you have chosen to use. Divide carefully into segments without breaking the inside skin. If you want to use grapes, remove each one from the bunch leaving a short stem attached. You can use more or less fruit, but allow ½ pt (250 ml) sugar syrup to each 1 lb (450 g) fruit.

To make the sugar syrup, dissolve the 12 oz (350 g) sugar in the water by heating in a large saucepan. When all sugar has dissolved bring rapidly to the boil and boil for 2 minutes. Put prepared fruit in a shallow bowl and pour syrup over while still warm. Cover and leave for 24 hours.

Pour off syrup and re-boil, adding another 2 oz (50 g) sugar. Pour over fruit again and leave for a further 24 hours. Repeat process 3 more times, adding 2 oz (50 g) extra sugar to syrup before each boiling. Drain syrup again and return it to pan, adding 3 oz (75 g) more sugar, and boil. When boiling add fruit and keep boiling for 3 minutes. Pour fruit and syrup back into dish and leave for 24 hours. Repeat boiling process with another 3 oz (75 g) sugar, then drain syrup from fruit thoroughly, using a wire cooling rack. To give a crisp finish to fruit, put rack into a cool oven 200°F (110°C) Gas Mark ¼ and leave oven door slightly ajar. Take out when crisp, and pack in airtight containers, until you want to use them, As well as serving as a sweetmeat, try as a dessert served chilled with whipped cream.

Candied Angelica

This is a very satisfying thing to do—to grow your own angelica in the garden and preserve it for decorating puddings and cakes. It is so expensive to buy already candied, and the process is extremely simple. However, you do need to leave the angelica and sugar to stand for 2 days.

Angelica   Granulated sugar

Choose young stems of angelica for preserving. Cut them into matching lengths and boil until tender. Remove from water and and strip off outer skin, then return to pan and simmer very slowly until they are green. You might have to add a little green food colouring at this point. Dry well and then weigh. Allow 1 lb (450 g) granulated sugar to each 1 lb (450 g) angelica. Place stems in a shallow dish and sprinkle sugar over them. Leave for 2 days and then boil sugar and stems well together. When thoroughly boiled, remove angelica and add 2 oz (50 g) granulated sugar to existing syrup. Boil this, then add angelica and boil for a further 5 minutes. Drain angelica and spread it on a tray in a cool oven to dry. Wrap in greaseproof paper and store in an airtight container until needed.

Candied Orange and Lemon Peel

Why not try making your own candied peel? It is very rewarding, cheap and quite delicious. It is also a way of using orange and lemon skins, after you have used the fruit and the juice. The candying process takes 2 days.

4 oranges $\frac{1}{2}$ oz (15 g) bicarbonate of soda
4 lemons $1\frac{1}{2}$ lb (675 g) granulated sugar

Remove all pulp and juice from the fruit. Keep skins in large pieces. Dissolve bicarbonate of soda in $\frac{1}{4}$ pt (150 ml) hot water and pour over each piece of peel. Add sufficient boiling water to cover peel completely. Allow to stand for 20 minutes. Rinse very well. Cover peel with cold water and bring to the boil. Simmer until tender. Make a sugar syrup from 1 lb (450 g) granulated sugar and $\frac{3}{4}$ pt (400 ml) water, by dissolving sugar in water over a gentle heat and then bringing to the boil. Pour this over peel and leave to stand for 2 days.

Strain off syrup and add a further $\frac{1}{2}$ lb (225 g) granulated sugar. Bring this slowly to the boil and simmer peel in it until peel looks clear. Lift peel out and dry it slowly on a baking tray in a cool oven.

Reduce syrup by boiling it gently for 30 minutes. Dip dried peel into syrup and dry again in oven. Boil up remaining syrup until it is cloudy and thick. Pour a very little into each piece of dried peel. Allow to dry again and then store in an airtight container until needed.

Christmas Gingerbread

Gingerbread has been associated with festive days since the Middle Ages. It was originally made with breadcrumbs flavoured with cinnamon, aniseed and ginger, and darkened with licorice and red wine. The ingredients were just stirred together, rolled thin and 'printed' with moulds, then dried in a cool oven—more like biscuits really. Later, it changed its nature and lost its breadcrumbs and was made of flour, sugar, butter, eggs and black treacle plus lots of spices—coriander, caraway seeds, cloves, mace, allspice, nutmeg, cinnamon and ginger. Candied orange, lemon and citron peel and other preserved fruits were added for flavouring and the mixture was made into small cakes or sweetmeats and baked in the oven. For special occasions, the gingerbread was covered with gold leaf or decorated with trefoils made of bay leaves and cloves. At Christmas, children were given dolls to represent Jesus made from gingerbread.

This recipe makes one large spongy gingerbread, which you can ice and decorate with crystallised fruit, silver and gold leaves, holly or whatever you like. Make it instead of (or in addition to!) a traditional Plum Cake.

8 oz (225 g) plain flour
½ teaspoon salt
1 teaspoon ground ginger
¼ teaspoon mixed spice
½ teaspoon bicarbonate of soda
½ teaspoon baking powder
3 oz (75 g) butter or margarine
4 oz (125 g) soft brown sugar
3 oz (75 g) black treacle
3 oz (75 g) golden syrup

¼ pt (150 ml) milk
1 egg, lightly beaten
2 oz (50 g) citron peel, chopped
2 oz (50 g) crystallised ginger, chopped
1 oz (25 g) blanched almonds, sliced
Grated rind of ½ lemon
½ teaspoon coffee essence

FOR GLAZING AND ICING:
Apricot jam, sieved
8 oz (225 g) icing sugar, sieved
2–3 tablespoons lemon juice

Crystallised or stem ginger or glacé cherries or any glacé fruits

Pre-set oven at 325°F (170°C) Gas Mark 3.

Grease and line an 8in (20cm) square cake tin with buttered greaseproof paper.

Sieve together flour and other dry ingredients. Gently warm butter, sugar, treacle and golden syrup. Make a well in centre of dry ingredients and add syrup mixture which should be just warm. Add warmed milk and lightly beaten egg. Mix and beat well. Beat in chopped peel, crystallised ginger, almonds, lemon rind and coffee essence. Pour mixture into tin. Bake in pre-heated cool oven 325°F (170°C) Gas Mark 3 for 45–60 minutes or when evenly risen and springy to the touch. Remove greaseproof paper and leave to cool. If your gingerbread should dip in the middle you have used too much treacle or syrup. To measure accurately, weigh a small basin or cup and then add syrup and weigh again. Syrup is easier to handle if slightly warmed.

To ice your gingerbread, warm some apricot jam and put through a sieve to make a glaze. Brush over top and sides of gingerbread (this will prevent the treacle seeping through and discolouring the icing). Leave to cool and set.

To make your icing, put sieved icing sugar and lemon juice in a small pan and heat, stirring until the mixture is warm (do not make the icing too hot). It should coat the back of a wooden spoon evenly, and look smooth and glossy. Pour over gingerbread leaving it to run slowly down the sides. Leave to cool and set.

Decorate with thinly sliced stem ginger and gold leaves and place on a gold doily—or decorate any way you choose (the more elaborate the gingerbread, the more traditional it is). This cake keeps extremely well in an airtight tin, and in fact has a better flavour if made at least a week in advance. It will also freeze very well.

Christmas Yule Log Cake

The Yule log is widely associated with Christmas Eve, the last day of preparation for the great festival. Traditionally a vast log was dragged to the kitchen hearthstone, where it burned throughout the festivities.

The Yule candle was usually lighted at the same time as the Yule log and placed in the centre of the dinner table where it had to remain without being moved, or snuffed, for the duration of the festivities, if evil was to be averted! It was often stood in an apple as a fertility symbol, to ensure a good harvest the following summer.

So why not make this very festive and delicious French cake as a treat for Christmas Eve or serve for tea on Christmas Day as a change from Christmas cake, or as well as!

1 oz (25 g) plain flour	2–3 drops of vanilla essence
1 dessertspoon cocoa	Small tin sweetened chestnut
Pinch of salt	purée
3 large eggs, separated	$\frac{1}{2}$ pt (250 ml) double cream,
Large pinch of cream of tartar	whipped
4 oz (125 g) caster sugar	Icing sugar

Pre-set oven at 325°F (170°C) Gas Mark 3. Grease and flour a swiss roll tin 8 x 12in (20 x 30cm). Sift flour with cocoa and salt. Whisk egg whites with cream of tartar until stiff; then gradually beat in half the sugar. Continue whisking until mixture looks very glossy and will stand in peaks.

Cream egg yolks until thick, then beat in remaining sugar and add vanilla essence. Stir sieved flour, cocoa and salt into yolks and pour this mixture over whites. Using a metal spoon cut and fold egg whites into rest of mixture gently, until thoroughly mixed. It is important to fold egg whites in lightly to keep in air and make sure your cake is not close-textured and biscuity, which apart from not tasting as good will make it impossible to roll up without cracking.

Turn mixture into prepared tin and cut through it gently several times to break up any large air bubbles which would result in large holes in the cake. Bake in pre-heated oven for 20–25 minutes, or until surface of cake springs back when gently pressed with fingertip.

Turn on to sheet of greaseproof paper dusted liberally with icing sugar and resting on a damp tea-towel. Trim edges of cake and roll up with tea-towel and greaseproof paper inside cake.

When cool, unroll cake carefully and spread the chestnut purée all over followed by the whipped cream. Roll up again, dust with more icing sugar for snow and decorate with a sprig of holly and a robin or glacé cherries and angelica.

Glazed Fruit Christmas Cake

If you would like a change from the dark, rich, traditional Christmas cake try this recipe. It keeps very well, so you can make it in October and ice in the normal way when you are ready.

8 oz (225 g) sultanas	Grated rind and juice of
3–4 tablespoons brandy or	1 lemon
sherry	Grated rind of 1 orange
4 oz (125 g) crystallised	4 eggs
pineapple	2 oz (50 g) ground almonds
2 oz (50 g) crystallised ginger	8 oz (225 g) plain flour
4 oz (125 g) glacé apricots	½ teaspoon salt
6 oz (175 g) glacé cherries,	4 oz (125 g) walnuts, chopped
washed	4 oz (125 g) candied peel
8 oz (225 g) unsalted butter	2 oz (50 g) angelica
8 oz (225 g) caster sugar	

Soak the sultanas in brandy for several hours or overnight if you can.
Pre-heat oven to 325°F (170°C) Gas Mark 3.

Prepare an 8in (20cm) round cake tin by greasing it with melted butter and lining with a double thickness of greaseproof paper brushed with melted butter. Tie a band of brown paper, standing about 1in (2·5cm) above the rim, round outside of tin.

Chop crystallised fruits and glacé apricots into smallish pieces, and quarter the cherries. Cream butter and sugar with lemon and orange rind until soft and fluffy. Beat eggs really hard until foamy and thick, and add to creamed mixture a little at a time, beating well between each addition. When all egg has been added, lightly fold in the ground almonds.

Sift flour with salt, and gently fold into creamed mixture. Stir in lemon juice and then prepared fruit, nuts, candied peel, angelica and sultanas soaked in brandy, a little at a time. Mixture should be moist enough to drop off a spoon if given a good shake. Add more brandy or sherry if it is not. Turn cake mixture into prepared tin and smooth over top making a hollow in the centre.

Bake at 325°F (170°C) Gas Mark 3 for 1 hour on shelf below centre of oven. After 1 hour, place a double sheet of greaseproof paper over the top of the tin and turn oven down to 300°F (150°C) Gas Mark 2 for a further 2–2¼ hours. The cake is done when it is evenly risen and brown and has shrunk a little from the sides of the tin. Leave cake in tin to cool, away from draughts. When completely cold, peel off paper, wrap in a double layer of greaseproof and store in an airtight tin. At odd intervals, make tiny holes in top and bottom of cake with a fine skewer and pour in some brandy.

Mince Pyes *(makes about 20)*

By Elizabethan times these had become part of traditional Christmas fare. They were known as 'shred' or 'minced' pies from the shredded meat in them. A typical Elizabethan recipe would be: 'Shred your meat, mutton or beef, and suet together fine. Season it with cloves, mace, pepper and some saffron, great raisins, currants and prunes. And so, put it into your pyes.' For many years afterwards, the pie filling was based on lean meat minced with an equal quantity of suet, and mixed with spices and dried fruit. In 1650 Oliver Cromwell passed an Act of Parliament authorising the imprisonment of anyone found guilty of eating a currant pie! Christmas Minced Pies were included—they were thought to be far too rich and indulgent and hinted at paganism.

After a few more decades, it was discovered that the suet, spices and fruit which now included apples as well as dried fruit, could be mixed with brandy or sack as long as 4 months in advance, and stored in stone jars, provided that the shredded meat was not added until just before the pies were made. From this it was only a short step to omitting the meat altogether which was already done during Lent anyway; hence our modern-day mince pie. Many myths and legends surround this Christmas pie. It was, and still is, considered essential by some people that twelve pies should be eaten between Christmas Day and Twelfth Day in order to ensure a lucky year. It's a good excuse anyway! They were originally oval in shape to represent the manger in which Jesus was laid and contained three spices as a reminder of gifts from the Three Kings. You can use shortcrust pastry but rich almond pastry does make a change.

52

12 oz (350 g) plain flour
8 oz (225 g) unsalted butter
3 oz (75 g) ground almonds

3 oz (75 g) caster sugar
2 egg yolks
2 tablespoons cold water

FOR THE FILLING AND THE TOPPING:
1 lb (450 g) homemade
mincemeat
2 tablespoons brandy or rum

1 egg white, beaten
Caster sugar

To make the pastry, sieve flour into a bowl. Rub in butter until mixture resembles breadcrumbs. Stir in ground almonds and sugar. Add egg yolks and enough cold water to make a firm paste. Cover and chill for 1 hour. Meanwhile, thoroughly mix the mincemeat with the brandy or rum, so that the flavour gets evenly distributed. Pre-set oven at 400°F (200°C) Gas Mark 6.

Roll out pastry to about $\frac{1}{8}$in (3mm) thick and cut half of it into 3in (7·5cm) rounds and half into 2$\frac{1}{2}$in (6cm) rounds with fluted pastry cutters. Grease 2$\frac{1}{2}$in (6cm) patty tins lightly, and line them with the 3in (7·5cm) rounds. Fill these with mincemeat to the level of the edges of the pastry. (Don't fill too much or the mincemeat will boil out over edges.)

Dip the smaller rounds of pastry into a little brandy mixed with milk and press lightly in position to form lids. Brush with beaten egg white, make a hole in centre of each pie and sprinkle with caster sugar. Bake fairly near top of oven for 25–30 minutes until golden brown. Cool on a wire rack and sprinkle with more caster sugar or sieved icing sugar. Store in an airtight tin until needed.

To serve, reheat in warm oven. Make sure you don't heat up too much, because mincemeat retains heat and can easily burn your mouth. Before serving, remove lids of mince pies and add a dollop of Brandy or Rum Butter (see recipes on pages 41 and 42) or clotted cream. Replace lids and serve on a gold-doily-covered plate decorated with holly and ribbon. Try serving on Christmas Eve with mulled wine or ale—delicious!

For a change, cook mince pies without lids and then pile a meringue mixture on top or make a Royal Mince Pie—a very old method of cooking one large pie topped with meringue. Brown under grill or in oven.

Mincemeat without Suet *(makes about 8 lb (3·6 kg))*
This is an unusual recipe using a large amount of cooking apples and no suet and includes cider and glacé cherries. Many people do not like the fattiness of suet, but love the richness of fruit. This is the recipe for them! It also keeps extremely well as the mincemeat is boiled before being packed into jars.

¾ pt (400 ml) medium or dry cider
1 lb (450 g) dark soft brown sugar
4 lb (1·8 kg) cooking apples
1 teaspoon mixed spice
1 teaspoon ground cinnamon
1 lb (450 g) currants

1 lb (450 g) stoned raisins
4 oz (125 g) glacé cherries, finely chopped
4 oz (125 g) blanched almonds, finely chopped
Finely grated rind and juice of 1 lemon
¼ pt (150 ml) brandy or rum

Put cider and sugar in a large saucepan and heat gently until sugar has dissolved. Peel, core and chop apples and add to pan. Stir in remaining ingredients, except for brandy or rum and bring slowly to boil, stirring all the time. Lower heat under saucepan, half-cover with a lid and simmer for about 30 minutes until mixture has become a soft pulp. Remove from heat and leave to get completely cold. Stir in brandy or rum. Spoon into clean dry screw-topped jars and cover with waxed circles before putting on lids. Store in a cool, dry place until Christmas.

Traditional Mincemeat *(makes about 8 lb (3·6 kg))*
1 lb (450 g) fresh beef suet
1 lb (450 g) cooking apples
8 oz (225 g) mixed candied peel
2 tablespoons sweet almonds
1 lb (450 g) stoned raisins
1 lb (450 g) sultanas
1 lb (450 g) currants

12 oz (350 g) brown sugar
1 teaspoon mixed spice
Grated rind and juice of 1 lemon
¼ pt (150 ml) rum, brandy or whisky

Remove skin and shred suet, dusting with a little flour to prevent it sticking. If you cannot buy butcher's suet use the packaged variety, but fresh certainly has a better flavour. Peel, core and chop apples coarsely. The best candied peel is sold in large pieces and you can buy a mixture of citron, lemon and orange peel. Remove any excess sugar before shredding as there is already sufficient in the recipe. This again has a much better flavour than packaged ready-chopped peel. How about making your own (see recipe on page 48)? It is well worth the effort as it is so expensive to buy.

Blanch and shred almonds. (Almonds are best bought with their skins on as they contain more oil. To blanch, pour boiling water over them in a basin and leave to cool.) The skins slip off easily when pressed with the fingers. Rinse in cold water to preserve their whiteness, dry and then shred. Mix suet, apple, candied peel and raisins together and pass through a mincer. Add remaining ingredients and mix well. Pack into clean, dry jars with screw-topped lids, covering top of mincemeat with a circle of waxed paper before putting on the lids. Store in a dry larder until required.

Traditional Plum Cake

Our rich dark Christmas cake is descended from the even richer and darker seventeenth-century 'Plumb Cake' which was given pride of place on every Christmas table. It was rich with butter and 'plumbs' (raisins), laced with spirits, and had 'marchpane' added as an icing. This elaborate almond paste and sugar confection fell from favour as a table centrepiece when the medieval banquet or side table of sweet dishes gave way to desserts as we know them, served at the main table. It was revived just as a decorative icing for rich cakes in the eighteenth century and has lasted until now as our modern-day almond paste.

Rich fruit cakes are best made at least eight weeks before they are needed, so particularly at Christmas time it is a good idea to make the Christmas cake in October or early November and then forget about it until you are ready to ice it.

12 oz (350 g) sultanas
12 oz (350 g) currants
8 oz (225 g) stoned raisins
6 oz (175 g) glacé cherries, rinsed and quartered or halved
4 oz (125 g) candied peel, finely chopped

Soak the above ingredients overnight in 3 tablespoons brandy, rum or sherry. The fruit will plumpen and absorb the spirit, and give extra flavour to your cake. You can use orange juice in exactly the same way if you prefer.

12 oz (350 g) unsalted butter
12 oz (350 g) soft brown sugar
6 eggs, beaten
12 oz (350 g) plain flour
Pinch of salt
1 teaspoon baking powder
1 teaspoon mixed spice
1 teaspoon grated nutmeg
1 teaspoon ground cinnamon

3 oz (75 g) blanched almonds, finely chopped
Finely grated rind and juice of 1 lemon
1 tablespoon brandy, rum or sherry
Vanilla, almond or ratafia essence

Pre-set oven at 325°F (170°C) Gas Mark 3. Grease a 10in (25cm) round cake tin or a 9in (23cm) square cake tin with melted butter and line with a double thickness of greaseproof paper. Brush this paper with melted butter also. Tie a double band of thick brown paper around the outside of the tin to protect the sides of the cake during baking.

Beat the butter until soft and light—unsalted butter gives a better flavour. Add the sugar, and cream together until *light, fluffy* and *white*. Add the beaten eggs a little at a time, beating well after each addition. If the mixture looks as if it might start curdling, add a little of the measured flour.

Sieve the flour with the salt, baking powder and spices into a large mixing bowl. Lightly fold this into the mixture a little at a time with a metal spoon, or you will end up with large holes in your cake. Stir in the fruit which has been soaking, and the almonds, and finally the lemon rind, juice, and a few drops of essence.

Spoon the mixture into the prepared cake tin and gently bang the tin on your work surface to disperse any air bubbles. Smooth the top, making a very slight depression in the centre. Dip your fingers in warm water and moisten the surface very slightly—just a film of water on the mixture. The small quantity of steam from this water during baking prevents a hard crust forming on the top of the cake.

Put the cake in the middle of the pre-heated oven and bake for $3\frac{1}{2}$ hours or until a trussing needle or fine skewer inserted in the centre comes out clean. Check the cake after 1 hour and cover with a square of double-thickness greaseproof paper or foil to prevent the top becoming too brown.

When cooked, remove from the oven and leave in the tin for at least 15 minutes to prevent cracking. Prick a few holes in the top of the cake and spoon over the tablespoon of chosen spirit. Leave until quite cold, then turn out of the tin and remove the greaseproof paper. Wrap the cake well in a large piece of double-thickness greaseproof paper secured with a large rubber band. Store in an airtight tin and every week or so make small holes with a fine skewer in the top and base of the cake and pour in teaspoonfuls of brandy, rum or sherry—all very alcoholic! If you don't have a large enough tin to store the cake, you can wrap it in foil, but always put it in greaseproof paper first, because the acid in the fruit can cause corrosion and mould can develop.

Store for at least 1 month and decorate as and when you choose.

Almond Paste

This recipe makes enough to cover the top and sides of a 10in (25cm) round cake. It has a particularly good flavour because orange-flower or rose water is added as it has been since the Middle Ages. This can be bought from any good grocer and is not expensive. A bottle will last you a long time, and adds just that little 'extra something' to many cold puddings and cakes.

12 oz (350 g) ground almonds
6 oz (175 g) caster sugar
6 oz (175 g) icing sugar,
  finely sieved
1 egg
1 tablespoon lemon juice
1 tablespoon brandy or sherry

$\frac{1}{2}$ teaspoon vanilla essence
$\frac{1}{4}$ teaspoon almond essence
2 teaspoons orange-flower or
  rose water
3 tablespoons apricot jam,
  warmed and sieved

Place the almonds, caster sugar and sieved icing sugar in a bowl and mix together. Whisk the egg with the lemon juice and other flavourings and add this to the almond mixture, pounding lightly to release some of the oil from the almonds. Knead lightly (with your hands dusted with icing sugar) until smooth. Be careful not to handle too much or the heat of your hands might make the paste too oily.

Brush the cake all over the sides and top thinly with the warmed apricot glaze. This coating makes sure that the almond paste will stick to the cake. Now place the paste on top of the cake; roll it over the top and down the sides.

Dust your hands with icing sugar again and smooth the paste firmly and evenly on to the sides of the cake. Turn it upside down and roll a rolling pin round the sides. This gives a clean, sharp edge to the paste. Turn the cake the right way up, level the top with the rolling pin and store wrapped in two layers of greaseproof paper in a tin for at least 1 week before icing. This gives the paste a chance to dry out, so that the oil from the almonds cannot seep through and discolour the icing, making it look rather dirty.

Any almond paste left over can be used for making marzipan fruits or for stuffing fresh dates—dip ends of date in melted plain chocolate after stuffing them—delicious!

Royal Icing

1 lb (450 g) icing sugar
2 egg whites
1 teaspoon glycerine

½ teaspoon orange-flower or rose water or a squeeze of lemon juice
Blue food colouring (optional)

Finely sieve the icing sugar. Whisk the egg whites in a clean grease-free bowl until frothy and add the icing sugar, one tablespoon at a time, beating thoroughly between each addition. Continue this beating until the mixture will stand in peaks, and is smooth and glossy. Stir in the glycerine and the flavouring. (The glycerine added to royal icing will prevent it from becoming very hard.) To improve the whiteness of the icing, add a tiny spot of edible blue colouring on the point of a skewer and beat it in very thoroughly; too much blue colouring will give the icing a greyish tint. Stir gently for a few minutes to reduce air bubbles.

Put the icing in an airtight container and cover with a lid, or cover the bowl with a damp cloth and place in a cool place. Leave to stand for several hours, preferably overnight. The next day, stir the icing gently to reduce the air bubbles. Use a dab of icing to fix the cake to a board and spread half of the remaining icing on the top and sides of the cake. Work the icing back and forth to get rid of any tiny air bubbles, then take a clean plastic ruler and holding it at each end glide it to and fro over the surface of the cake until you have a smooth finish. Use the same method to smooth over the sides. Now leave the cake for 24 hours for the icing to dry.

Next day use the rest of your icing for piping or whatever decoration you decide on. If you are running short of time or don't really enjoy icing, try piling small coloured Christmas tree baubles in the centre of your cake fixing them with icing, and cutting out leaves from silver or gold doilies to place round the edge of your cake. It really will look stunning and very unusual.

Glacé Fruit Topping

A lot of people don't like iced fruit cakes, so why not try this glacé fruit topping. It is also a very quick and attractive way of decorating the Christmas cake, if you are short of time.

8 oz (225 g) apricot jam
Juice of 1 lemon
4 oz (125 g) glacé pineapple
  rings or chunks
4 oz (125 g) red glacé cherries

4 oz (125 g) green and yellow
  glacé cherries
4 oz (125 g) angelica
4 oz (125 g) Brazil nuts and
  walnuts

Place the apricot jam and lemon juice in a pan. Warm, stirring all the time. Rub through a sieve and brush this apricot glaze all over the top of your cake. Arrange the pineapple rings or chunks (dipped first in the apricot jam) in a row across the centre of the cake. Fill the centres of the rings with cherries and decorate with angelica leaves. Arrange the rest of the fruit and nuts in rows either side of the pineapple rings, dipping each piece in the glaze before fixing on the cake. Give a final brushing all over the fruit with more apricot glaze. Leave until cold, and then store in an airtight tin in a cool place until required. If you want, you can make a little glacé icing by mixing icing sugar, brandy and water together, and trickle this over the glacé fruits before serving.

To serve, tie a wide satin ribbon around your cake and place on a gold- or silver-doily covered plate.

NEW YEAR'S EVE

The Scots have their own customs for greeting and toasting the first day of the year, but all over the rest of Britain the New Year should be greeted by a tall dark stranger who should enter the house with gifts symbolic of food, drink and warmth, and then pass right through the house. If the 'first-footer' is a dark man, then the household will have good fortune for the rest of the coming year, but if, on the other hand, the first person to pass over the threshold is fair, or female, dark or fair, then ill fortune will follow. If a bough of mistletoe is given to the first cow to calve after New Year's day the rest of the herd will be safeguarded from ill luck throughout the year.

Agnes' New Year Shortbread (*makes 16 pieces*)
No Scottish Hogmanay is complete without shortbread when it is always offered to 'first-footers'. In fact it is eaten during the festive season between Christmas Eve and Hogmanay. True shortbread is thick and not rolled out into biscuits, and so delicious. I have found this recipe most successful—it was given to me by a Scottish friend.

8 oz (225 g) unsalted butter	4 oz (125 g) cornflour
4 oz (125 g) icing sugar, sieved	1 teaspoon rose water (optional)
8 oz (225 g) plain flour	caster sugar for sprinkling

Pre-set oven at 300°F (150°C) Gas Mark 2.
    Blend butter and icing sugar together in a bowl with as little working as possible to avoid oiliness. Your utensils should be cold. (Excellent shortbread is made in the Shetlands, because of the cool climate.) Sieve flours together and gradually work into butter mixture with rose water. Gently press paste (making sure your hands are cold) into 2 shortbread moulds, if you have them, or a swiss roll tin or 2 x 7in (18cm) sandwich tins. Prick all over with a fork to stop it rising. Mark round edges with handle of a fork or pinch them using your thumb and first finger. Dust with caster sugar and bake on lowest shelf in oven for 45–60 minutes, or until shortbread is very pale brown. Remove from oven and mark into slices with back of knife, forking a pattern on the top if you wish. Leave to cool in tin before cutting slices through. Dust with more caster sugar and store in an airtight tin until needed.

Shortbread freezes well. To use, refresh from frozen loosely covered with foil, in oven at 350°F (180°C) Gas Mark 4 for about 10 minutes.

Variations:

Glacé Cherry Shortbread

Add 4 oz (125 g) roughly chopped glacé cherries to butter and sugar mixture and then work in flours plus 1 teaspoon mixed spice. Decorate with 2 oz (50 g) halved glacé cherries before baking.

This variation looks very Christmassy.

Hazelnut Shortbread

Add 4 oz (125 g) roughly chopped hazelnuts or blanched almonds to butter and sugar mixture and work in flours. Decorate with whole nuts pressed into paste before baking.

Orange Shortbread

Add grated rind of 2 oranges to butter and sugar mixture and work in flours. Decorate with pieces of candied orange peel, and bake.

Iced Orange Shortbread

Add grated rind of 2 oranges to butter and sugar mixture and work in flours. Bake, then allow to cool a little. Sprinkle with 2 oz (50 g) finely chopped walnuts. Mix together 4 oz (125 g) sifted icing sugar with 4 tablespoons fresh orange juice. Drizzle this evenly over shortbread and leave to cool completely.

Almond Shortbread

Add 3 oz (75 g) ground almonds to butter and sugar mixture. Work in flours and add almond essence to taste.

This variation is a very good one to serve with syllabubs, fruit fools and creams.

Ginger Shortbread

Add chopped stem ginger to butter mixture and work in flours plus 1 teaspoon or more of ground ginger.

Black Bun

A bun is an old Scottish word for a plum cake and is a very dark rich fruit cake made traditionally for Hogmanay or New Year's Day, although it was formerly eaten on Twelfth Night. The cake is encased in a pastry shell during baking to keep the juices and flavour from escaping. This original bread paste was discarded when the cake was eaten, but later the pastry was made with fat and became much more edible. At Hogmanay gatherings, great slices of Black

Bun are traditionally washed down with many 'Het Pints'—spiced ale mixed with eggs and whisky. This brew used to be carried through the streets in great copper kettles to welcome in the New Year.

FOR THE PASTRY CASE:

1 lb (450 g) plain flour
Pinch of salt
½ teaspoon baking powder

7 oz (200 g) butter
About 6 tablespoons iced water
Beaten egg to glaze

To make the pastry, sift flour, salt and baking powder into a bowl. Rub in butter to make a consistency like breadcrumbs. Add just sufficient iced water to make a stiff paste with a knife and knead lightly. Shape into a ball and wrap in cling-film. Leave in refrigerator for at least 30 minutes. Bring to room temperature and then roll out on a floured board. Use two-thirds of the pastry to line a greased 2 lb (1 kg) loaf tin.

FOR THE FILLING:

6 oz (175 g) plain flour
2 teaspoons allspice
1 teaspoon ground cinnamon
1 teaspoon ground mixed spice
½ teaspoon freshly milled
   black pepper
½ teaspoon baking powder
¼ teaspoon cream of tartar
Generous pinch of salt
3 oz (75 g) soft dark brown sugar

12 oz (350 g) seedless raisins
1 lb (450 g) currants
2 oz (50 g) blanched almonds,
   chopped
2 oz (50 g) candied peel,
   chopped
1 egg
2 tablespoons brandy or rum
3 tablespoons milk
Caster sugar for sprinkling

Pre-set oven at 325°F (170°C) Gas Mark 3.

To make the filling, sift flour with spices, pepper, baking powder, cream of tartar and salt. Stir in sugar, dried fruit, nuts and peel. Add beaten egg, brandy and milk to moisten mixture. Pack into pastry case and smooth top. Roll out remaining pastry and use to make a lid. Dampen edges with milk and press together well. Prick all over with a fork and pierce right through to base of tin a few times with a skewer. Brush with beaten egg and bake in pre-heated oven for 2 hours, then reduce heat to 300°F (150°C) Gas Mark 2 for a further 1 hour. The bun is cooked when a thin skewer, inserted carefully through top crust into filling, comes out clean.

Cool and store in an airtight tin at least 2 weeks before cutting. Sprinkle with caster sugar before serving.

New Year Godcakes (*makes about 8*)

These triangular mincemeat puffs have been made in the Coventry area since the Middle Ages. Traditionally they were given to godchildren by their godparents as a New Year gift for good luck.

They were known both to the very poor and the rich, but they varied in size according to the prosperity, or otherwise, of the giver.

1½ lb (675 g) prepared puff
  pastry
1 lb (450 g) homemade
  mincemeat

1 egg white
Caster or icing sugar

Pre-set oven at 425°F (220°C) Gas Mark 7.

Roll out puff pastry on a floured board to about ⅛in (3mm) thick and cut into oblong shapes about 6 x 8in (15 x 20cm). Put a generous spoonful of mincemeat in centre of each. Fold pastry over to make an elongated triangle, moisten edges and press well together. Turn over and make 3 small slits (said to represent the Trinity). Repeat with remaining pastry oblongs. Place on a dampened baking tray, and bake in hot oven for about 15 minutes until well risen and golden.

Meanwhile, whisk egg white until frothy. When cakes are cooked, brush tops with egg white and sprinkle with caster sugar or sifted icing sugar. Return to oven for about 3 minutes until shiny. Cool on a wire rack and eat as soon as possible or tops will become damp.

Petticoat Tails (*makes 12 pieces*)
These are a kind of shortbread but slightly thinner and crisper than the traditional shortbread. Their fascinating name may come from the French 'petites gatelles' meaning 'small cakes', or from the fact that their shape resembled the stiffened hoop petticoats that were once worn by ladies to hold out their skirts.

8 oz (225 g) plain flour
Pinch of salt
1½ oz (40 g) caster sugar
2 tablespoons milk

4 oz (125 g) unsalted butter
A few caraway seeds (optional)
Caster sugar for sprinkling

Pre-set oven at 325°F (160°C) Gas Mark 3.

Sift flour and salt into a bowl. Stir in sugar. Heat milk and butter together until butter has dissolved. Pour into flour mixture and work with your hand to form a smooth paste. (Work in caraway seeds here, if you like them.) Turn out on to a floured board and knead lightly. Roll out and cut into a round about 8in (20cm) in diameter then place on a baking tray lined with non-stick bakewell paper. Cut out a round about 2in (5cm) in diameter from the centre, then mark into 8 portions from outer edge to centre ring.

Bake in pre-heated oven for 30–40 minutes. Petticoat tails should be browned a little more than traditional shortbread. (You can bake the cut-out biscuit at the same time.) Cool on a wire rack. When crisp sprinkle with caster sugar and store in airtight tin until required.

TWELFTH NIGHT

Twelfth Night, 6 January, is sometimes called Twelfth-Day Eve, Eve of the Epiphany, or Old Christmas Eve. It was in fact the latter before the calendar was changed and Old Twelfth Night was 17 January. The festival commemorates the visit of the Magi to the Christ Child, and Twelfth Day used to be celebrated to the same extent as Christmas Day.

Twelfth Night is the start of the period when farmers used to wassail their orchards to ensure a good harvest, and fires used to be lit to bring success to the farm, dairy and orchard. Preparations for the revel included making a large, rich Twelfth Night Cake in which a bean and a pea were inserted before baking. He who received the slice containing the bean was elected King of the Bean and she who received the slice containing the pea was elected Queen and they both enjoyed regal honours during the revel.

It was also customary to bake a large Twelfth Night Pie which was cut open to reveal a flock of live birds, or a number of frogs, or even a small human being! Such pies were made of coarse paste filled with bran and yellowed over with saffron or yolks of eggs. After baking, the bran was removed and the livestock introduced through holes in the bottom crust. They were then produced to 'cause much delight and pleasure to the whole company'.

Christmas decorations are now usually left up until Twelfth Night, after which it is considered unlucky not to remove them.

Twelfth Night Cake

To carry on the tradition, bury a dried bean and pea in this rich fruit cake and have some fun!

8 oz (225 g) unsalted butter
8 oz (225 g) caster sugar
4 eggs
3 tablespoons brandy or rum
8 oz (225 g) plain flour
$\frac{1}{4}$ teaspoon ground cinnamon
$\frac{1}{4}$ teaspoon freshly grated
   nutmeg

8 oz (225 g) currants
8 oz (225 g) seedless raisins
4 oz (125 g) sultanas
3 oz (75 g) blanched almonds,
   chopped
1 dried pea and 1 dried bean

Pre-set oven at 300°F (150°C) Gas Mark 2. Grease and line a 10in (25cm) round cake tin with buttered greaseproof paper.

Cream butter and sugar until light and fluffy. Whisk eggs with brandy or rum and beat gradually into creamed mixture. Sift flour and spices and add a little at a time together with fruit and nuts. Put mixture into prepared cake tin and smooth top, making a slight hollow in centre and inserting pea and bean if you wish. Tie a double band of brown paper around tin and bake in pre-heated oven for 3–3$\frac{1}{2}$ hours. If top of cake is getting too brown, cover with a sheet of greaseproof paper. Cake is cooked when a thin skewer inserted in centre comes out clean. Leave to cool in tin for 15 minutes and then complete cooling on a wire rack.

Serve cake decorated with a gold paper frill around it to represent the crown of the Magi.

Twelfth Night Pie *(serves 6)*

Traditionally, silver trinkets and charms were put in this pie, and the person who was served the slice with the trinket was supposed to have good luck throughout the year. If you want to stay with tradition wrap a coin or charm in foil and bury in the pie before putting on the pastry lid.

8 oz (225 g) dried apricots
$\frac{3}{4}$ pt (400 ml) water
4 oz (125 g) sugar
1 vanilla pod, pierced
12 oz (350 g) plain flour, sifted
Pinch of salt

3 oz (75 g) caster or icing sugar
Grated rind of 1 lemon
6 oz (175 g) butter
2 egg yolks
4 tablespoons iced water
Beaten egg to glaze

Soak dried apricots in water overnight. Next day, cook apricots over a low heat in soaking liquor with sugar and vanilla pod, for 20 minutes.

Meanwhile, prepare pastry by placing sifted flour and salt in mixing bowl. Stir in sugar and grated lemon rind. Rub in butter until mixture resembles breadcrumbs. Mix egg yolks and water together and work into dough with a knife. Knead pastry on a floured board and form into a ball. Leave in refrigerator for 30 minutes, wrapped in cling film or a polythene bag.

Pre-set oven at 400°F (200°C) Gas Mark 6. Remove vanilla pod from apricots and reduce, by heating, to a purée. Bring pastry to room temperature, divide into 2 pieces and roll out on a floured board fairly thinly. Line a 9in (23cm) flan tin with half the pastry. Fill with puréed apricots and put in your charm. Top with second half of pastry, pressing edges firmly together. Brush with beaten egg and make swirls from centre of pie to edge, with a small knife, to look a bit like the rays of the sun. Bake in pre-heated oven for about 30 minutes, then reduce to a moderate oven 350°F (180°C) Gas Mark 4 for 20 minutes longer or until pie is golden brown. (Cover with foil if getting too brown.)

Serve warm or cold with whipped cream sweetened with a little apricot brandy or a hard sauce like Brandy or Rum Butter (see recipes on pages 41 and 42). Decorate with gold leaves and serve on a gold-paper doily.

Wassail

The word 'wassail' comes from the Old English salutation 'wes hal' meaning 'Be of good health'. It was customary to wassail the apple trees in the orchard on the twelve days of Christmas to ensure a bountiful apple crop. This was common in all apple-growing areas, but now survives chiefly in Devon and Somerset on Twelfth Night, 6 January, and in a few parishes in the West Country on Old Twelfth Night, 17 January. One of the best apple-bearing trees is chosen by the owner, and his labourers and their families gather round it after dusk, with shotguns and a large bowl of wassail or cider. The shotguns are fired through the branches to raise the sleeping tree spirit and drive away the demons of bad luck lurking around the tree's topmost branches. Sometimes the women have taken pots and pans to bang to make sure the demons are driven off! A little wassail is poured around the roots and a piece of toast, soaked in wassail, is placed in a fork of the tree. A toast to the tree is drunk by all present including the children and sometimes, to make extra sure of a good crop, some of the branches are pulled down and next year's fruit buds dipped in the wassail bowl. While all this is taking place the Wassail Song is sung, asking the trees to bear heavy crops of big apples.

3 small red apples

3 tablespoons soft brown sugar

$\frac{1}{2}$ teacup brown ale

2 pt (1·25 l) brown ale

$\frac{1}{2}$ pt (150 ml) sweet sherry

$\frac{1}{4}$ teaspoon cinnamon

$\frac{1}{4}$ teaspoon nutmeg

$\frac{1}{4}$ teaspoon ginger

Thin strip of lemon rind

Soft brown sugar to taste

Slices of brown toast

Slit skin round centre of apples with a sharp knife. Bake in oven with sugar and $\frac{1}{2}$ teacup brown ale, basting well until apples are soft.

Meanwhile, in a large saucepan, heat 2 pt (1·25 l) brown ale with the sherry, spices and lemon rind. Simmer for 5 minutes. Add baked apples to ale, with more brown sugar to taste. Serve very hot in a punch bowl with small pieces of toast floating on surface.

SHROVE TUESDAY

Shrove Tuesday precedes the first day of Lent—between 2 February and 8 March, and was the day the parish priest would hear confession from his parishioners. The long Lenten fast was ushered in by a hearty indulgence in pancakes on Shrove Tuesday using up all the eggs, butter and milk before the fasting commenced. The cook used to set aside the first three pancakes she made: 'One for Peter, two for Paul and three for Him who made us all.' Each single girl would make a pancake and feed it to the rooster. The number of hens that joined him would be the number of years before she would marry. The day was also a popular one for cockfighting.

Pancake races are still very popular in various parts of England. The original race is believed to have started sometime in the fifteenth century when a busy housewife, hearing the Shrove Tuesday noontide church bell ring, was so anxious not to be late for the service, that she rushed out of her house with her frying pan plus a sizzling pancake in her hand! That church bell is now called the Pancake Bell and is rung at the start of the races. The winner receives a prayer book.

Nowadays, few people fast during Lent, but the custom of eating pancakes on Shrove Tuesday still survives.

Traditional Pancakes (*makes 10–12*)

The controversy over the respective merits of pancake batters mixed with milk or with water has raged since medieval days, but by the eighteenth century milk was generally used. Sometimes extra rich batters were made by the addition of cream, brandy, sherry or sack. I find that a mixture of half milk, half water gives excellent results. The secret of making good pancakes lies in using a good quality, heavy-based pan, and it is a good idea to keep one pan specially for cooking pancakes.

4 oz (125 g) plain flour
½ teaspoon salt
1 egg, beaten
¼ pt (150 ml) milk
¼ pt (150 ml) cold water

2 tablespoons cooking oil or
   lard
Lemon juice
Caster sugar, for sprinkling
3 lemons, quartered

To make batter, sieve flour and salt into a mixing bowl. Make a well in centre and pour in beaten egg. Mix together the milk and water and gradually beat in half this liquid until a thick batter is formed. Pour in remaining liquid and 1 teaspoon of cooking oil. Beat until smooth. Leave to stand in refrigerator for 1 hour.

Heat a little of remaining oil or lard in a 7in (18cm) pancake or frying pan and when very hot, pour in about 2 tablespoons batter (your pancakes should be paper thin). Tilt pan quickly so that batter runs over bottom of pan. Cook over high heat until the underside is golden brown. Toss pancake or turn over with a palette knife and cook other side until golden brown. Slide pancake on to kitchen paper or a clean tea-towel on a hot plate and keep warm while cooking the remaining pancakes.

To serve, sprinkle each pancake with sugar and lemon juice to taste, roll up and arrange on a warmed serving platter. Sprinkle with more caster sugar. Place lemon quarters around edge of platter.

Pancakes will freeze extremely well. Pile up with foil between each pancake, then wrap in freezer bag or foil. Seal, label and freeze. To thaw, unwrap and leave at room temperature for about 20 minutes, and reheat in oven.

Variations:

With Honey and Walnut Sauce

Make pancakes as before. Melt 1 oz (25 g) butter in a frying pan and add 1 rounded tablespoon thick honey, juice of ½ lemon and 10 oz (275 g) chopped walnuts. Stir until blended. Slide one pancake into mixture, fold in half and in half again. Slide in next pancake and repeat until all your pancakes are used up. Arrange on a heated serving dish, and pour any remaining nut mixture over the top. Serve immediately.

68

With Apple and Calvados
Cook pancakes as before. Peel, core and thinly slice 6 dessert apples. Fry in 2 oz (50 g) hot butter for about 10 minutes until soft and pale brown, then add 3 tablespoons sugar and 4 tablespoons double cream. Remove from heat and stir well. Spread some of apple filling on each pancake, roll up and arrange on an ovenproof dish. Reheat for 5 minutes in oven at 400°F (200°) Gas Mark 6, sprinkle with 6 tablespoons Calvados sweetened with 1 tablespoon sugar, and set alight. (You can use any spirit in place of Calvados.)

With Orange and Grand Marnier
Whisk grated rind and juice of 1 orange, 3 eggs, and 6 oz (175 g) sugar together. Heat in a bowl over saucepan of boiling water until thick. Remove from heat before it boils. Stir in 2 oz (50 g) butter and 2 tablespoons Grand Marnier (or Cointreau). Spread a little of this filling on to each cooked pancake and fold into four. Serve with clotted cream.

With Apricots and Brandy
Poach 1 lb (450 g) fresh apricots gently with 2 tablespoons lemon juice, 1 tablespoon brandy, ½ pt (250 ml) water and 4 oz (125 g) sugar until soft and pulpy. Cook pancakes as before, and put a little filling in each. Roll up and place in a warmed serving dish. Spoon over any remaining filling, and sprinkle with flaked almonds. Reheat for 5 minutes in oven at 400°F (200°C) Gas Mark 6. Serve hot with pouring cream.

(You can use tinned apricots—leave out water in this case, and add sugar to taste.)

With Apricot Preserve and Ratafias
Cook pancakes as before. Sprinkle each one with a few crumbled ratafias or macaroons. Spread on a good dollop of apricot or other fruit preserve. Serve immediately with whipped or clotted cream.

With Blackberries and Clotted Cream
Cook pancakes as before. Spread each with a little clotted cream, cover with fresh or frozen blackberries, sprinkle with caster sugar and a little lemon juice. Roll up neatly and place in an ovenproof dish. Heat through in oven at 400°F (200°C) Gas Mark 6 for 5 minutes. Serve hot, dredged with caster sugar and more clotted cream.

Quire of Paper

This method of serving wafer-thin cream pancakes was admired during the eighteenth century. The batter was run as thinly as possible over the bottom of the pan and cooked on one side only. The finished pancakes were dredged with caster sugar and laid one on top of the other until a pile of twenty was made. Sherry or sack was often served with the pancakes, along with melted butter.

4 oz (125 g) plain flour	Sherry
1 oz (25 g) caster sugar	Unsalted butter for frying
2 eggs and 2 extra yolks	Redcurrant jelly
¼ pt (150 ml) single cream	Clotted cream
¼ pt (150 ml) milk	

Sieve flour and sugar into a bowl. Beat whole eggs, egg yolks, cream and milk together. Pour into well in centre of dry ingredients and beat until you have a smooth batter. Add enough sherry to give the consistency of thin cream. Heat a heavy-bottomed pancake pan, brush with melted butter and fry pancakes in same way as in previous recipes.

Make a stack of pancakes—about 15, spreading each with a little redcurrant jelly and clotted cream. To serve, cut into wedges like a cake. Dredge with caster or icing sugar.

Ashover Pancakes (*serves 6–8*)

It is said that these were made to celebrate the massacre of Danish invaders on one particular Ash Wednesday in Saxon times. Some people believe that this ancient recipe for pancakes was the ancestor of the later Shrove Tuesday or pre-Lenten pancakes. It is still used in parts of Nottinghamshire.

1 lb (450 g) plain flour	2 oz (50 g) shredded beef suet
½ teaspoon bicarbonate of soda	2 eggs, beaten
1 teaspoon cream of tartar	Fat or oil to deep-fry
4 teaspoons baking powder	

Sift dry ingredients into a bowl. Stir in suet and add eggs. Mix to a firm dough. Divide into balls the size of a walnut and fry, a few at a time, in deep hot fat, until golden brown. Drain well on kitchen paper and place in an ovenproof dish. Heat through in a cool oven at 300°F (150°C) Gas Mark 2 for a few minutes until softened.

Serve hot with jam or syrup and caster sugar.

Sugar and Spice Doughnuts (*makes 20*)

Doughnuts were traditional fare on Shrove Tuesday, as well as pancakes, and for the same reason. They were made with jam or fruit, plain or heavily spiced. This recipe is for ring doughnuts, deep-fried and tossed in sugar and spice.

1 lb (450 g) self-raising flour

Pinch of salt

8 oz (225 g) caster sugar

6 oz (175 g) soft margarine

2 large eggs, beaten

A little milk to mix

Oil or fat for deep-frying

1 teaspoon ground nutmeg

1 teaspoon ground cinnamon

Sift flour and salt into a bowl. Stir in 2 oz (50 g) sugar. Rub in margarine and mix to a stiff dough with eggs and milk. Roll out on a floured board to ¼in (½cm) thick and cut into 3in (7·5cm) rounds with a plain cutter. Cut out centres of each doughnut using a 1in (2·5cm) plain cutter. Deep-fry in hot oil or fat for about 5 minutes until golden brown and well risen. Drain on kitchen paper.

Mix remaining sugar with spices and toss doughnuts in this mixture to coat well.

MOTHERING SUNDAY

The fourth Sunday in Lent is commonly known as Mothering Sunday or Mother's Day, because this was the one day in the year when the older children working away from home in domestic service were allowed time off to return home and possibly attend their mother church with the rest of the family, as was customary on this day. The children were allowed to bake a large cake to take home as a gift to their mothers—the traditional Simnel Cake. This was needed to feed the visiting offspring and other relatives. Young married couples also made a practice of visiting their parents' homes on this day.

The family were allowed a slight lapse in the austere Lenten fast and feasted on Roast Loin of Veal, or a stuffed bacon joint, and Fig Pudding or Pie, Cheesecakes and 'Frumenty'. The latter was simply boiled wheat cooked again in milk with dried fruit, sugar and spices and was eaten all over Britain.

Orange-Stuffed Roast Loin of Veal (serves 6)
Veal is a dry meat and must be roasted slowly and with plenty of fat. It should never be overdone or subjected to fierce heat at the start of cooking as is red meat.

3 lb (1·4 kg) loin of veal,
  boned and rolled
1 medium cooking apple
1 small onion, chopped
Rind of 1 orange, grated
Flesh of 2 oranges, chopped
2 oz (50 g) fresh white
  breadcrumbs
1 tablespoon fresh parsley,
  chopped

Salt
Freshly ground black pepper
1 egg, beaten
6 rashers green streaky bacon
Dripping
½ pt (250 ml) water
Glazed orange slices for
  garnishing

Pre-set oven at 375°F (190°C) Gas Mark 5.

Open out joint and season inside lightly. Peel, core and chop apple and combine with chopped onion, orange rind and flesh, breadcrumbs, parsley and season to taste. Bind together with egg. Spread over veal, roll up and secure with skewers and string. Weigh

72

joint and place in roasting tin. Lay bacon over joint and spread liberally with dripping. Season with salt and pepper. Add water to roasting tin. Cook in pre-heated oven allowing 40 minutes per 1 lb (450 g) plus 40 minutes over. Baste joint every 15 minutes or so. Add more water if joint gets dry.

To glaze orange slices, put them in roasting tin with joint for the last 15 minutes of cooking time. Serve joint garnished with glazed orange slices and with thin gravy made from pan juices. Further garnish with sprigs of parsley or watercress.

English Saucer Cheesecakes (*serves 4*)

These cheesecakes were traditionally eaten when the family gathered together to celebrate Mothering Sunday. They were usually served with a stuffed bacon joint.

4 oz (125 g) rich shortcrust pastry	Grated rind of $\frac{1}{2}$ lemon
4 oz (125 g) curd cheese	3 egg yolks
2 oz (50 g) caster sugar	1 oz (25 g) candied peel, chopped
Pinch of salt	2 oz (50 g) raisins, stoned
$\frac{1}{4}$ level teaspoon grated nutmeg	(optional)

Pre-set oven at 350°F (180°C) Gas Mark 4.

Roll out pastry on a floured board and cut into 4 circles to line 4 saucers or Yorkshire pudding tins. Combine curd cheese with sugar, salt, nutmeg and lemon rind. Beat in egg yolks to give a stiff mixture. Divide peel and raisins (if using them) between pastry cases and spread curd mixture over. Bake in pre-heated oven for about 25 minutes until golden. Serve warm.

Mothering Sunday Wafers (*makes about 15*)

Wafers have been made since medieval days. In Georgian times the practice of rolling them off hot wafer irons on to small sticks was introduced so they were in a curled form when put to cool. This helped to make them crisper. Wafers were eaten at the main meal until the eighteenth century when they appeared on the tea-table especially on Mothering Sunday. Brandy snaps are modern descendants of the rolled wafer.

4 oz (125 g) plain flour	4 tablespoons double cream
3 oz (75 g) caster sugar	2 tablespoons orange-flower water

Pre-set oven at 400°F (200°C) Gas Mark 6.

Sift flour into a bowl, add sugar and stir in cream and orange-flower water. Beat thoroughly with an electric hand whisk for 6 minutes, or longer if you are beating by hand, until completely smooth. Spread spoonfuls of the mixture very thinly on greased baking trays. Bake in pre-heated oven for 6–8 minutes, until pale golden in colour. Leave for a few seconds, then remove from the tray and curl each wafer round a rolling pin until firm. If they harden before curling, place baking tray in oven for a few seconds to soften wafers again. Cool on a wire rack. When cold, wafers should be curved in shape and very crisp. Serve for tea, or with fruit creams, syllabubs or ice-cream.

Spiced Fig Pudding (*serves 6*)

This is an another recipe traditionally associated with Mothering Sunday, particularly in the North of England. A similar pudding was eaten in the South on Palm Sunday. This custom was said to be connected with the Gospel account of the barren fig tree. Few figs are harvested in England nowadays, as they are often difficult to ripen here; so this recipe uses dried figs soaked overnight. It can of course be made with fresh ones if available, in which case they should be stewed until tender.

6 oz (175 g) dried figs, soaked overnight	4 oz (125 g) shredded suet
2 oz (50 g) self-raising flour	8 oz (225 g) dates, stoned and chopped
½ teaspoon mixed spice	3 oz (75 g) raisins
Freshly grated nutmeg	Grated rind and juice of
6 oz (175 g) fresh white breadcrumbs	1 orange
2 oz (50 g) preserved ginger, chopped	2 large eggs
	2 tablespoons brandy or sherry

After soaking overnight, chop figs. Sift flour together with spice into a mixing bowl. Add breadcrumbs, suet, chopped ginger, fruit and orange rind. Mix everything together very thoroughly. Beat eggs with brandy or sherry, and orange juice. Add to mixture, stirring well to combine all ingredients. Put mixture into a well-buttered 1½ pt (750 ml) pudding basin. Cover with buttered greaseproof paper and pudding cloth or foil (with a pleat at centre to allow pudding to rise). Secure with string and steam for 4 hours.

Turn out and serve hot with homemade custard. This pudding is also delicious with Brandy and Lemon Butter (page 41), or Rum and Orange Butter (page 42) or Rum Sauce (page 44).

Simnel Cake

Nowadays, we think of the Simnel Cake as an Easter speciality, but traditionally it was made for Mothering Sunday or mid-Lent Sunday. It was common to start baking Simnel Cakes shortly after Christmas, as slices were often sent to relatives overseas.

.

Simnels were made in medieval times, but were light biscuity confections, which had to be boiled before they were baked. This medieval Simnel died out in the late seventeenth century and its name was transferred to the rich raised fruit cake baked for mid-Lent. This cake had a paste crust made of fine flour (hence the name Simnel, from the Latin word for fine flour, which is 'simila') and water, coloured a deep yellow with saffron. The crust was filled with a rich plum cake mixture which included figs, representing 'fruitfulness in offspring'. Plenty of candied lemon peel and other goodies were piled on top of the cake mixture. Almond paste has taken the place of the paste crust.

8 oz (225 g) plain flour
2 oz (50 g) rice flour
Large pinch of salt
1 teaspoon mixed spice
Large pinch of baking powder
8 oz (225 g) butter
Grated rind of 2 lemons
8 oz (225 g) caster sugar

4 eggs, separated
4 oz (125 g) currants, washed
8 oz (225 g) sultanas, washed
4 oz (125 g) glacé cherries, rinsed and halved
1 oz (25 g) candied peel, chopped

FOR THE ALMOND PASTE FILLING AND TOPPING:

12 oz (350 g) ground almonds
12 oz (350 g) icing sugar, sieved
3 large egg yolks
2 teaspoons lemon juice
½ teaspoon almond essence
½ teaspoon vanilla essence

About 1 tablespoon orange-flower water, brandy or sherry
1 dessertspoon apricot jam or redcurrant jelly
1 small egg, beaten
Caster sugar for sprinkling

First make the almond paste. Place almonds and sifted icing sugar in a bowl and mix together. Whisk egg yolks with lemon juice, essences and orange-flower water, brandy or sherry. Stir this into the almond and sugar mixture and knead to a stiff smooth paste. Store in greaseproof paper in a cool place until needed.

Pre-set oven at 350°F (180°C) Gas Mark 4. Prepare an 8in (20cm) round cake tin by brushing with melted butter and lining with greaseproof paper, also brushed with fat.

To make the cake, sift the flours with the salt, spice and baking powder into a large bowl. Cream butter with lemon rind until soft, add sugar and continue creaming until mixture is light and fluffy. Separate eggs and beat yolks into mixture. Whip egg whites until stiff.

Fold one third of the sifted flour into the mixture and then fold in egg whites alternately with remaining flour and dried fruit, glacé cherries, and peel. Put half mixture into prepared cake tin, spreading it a little up the sides.

Take just over one third of the almond paste, roll it into a smooth round, place it in tin on top of cake mixture. Cover with remaining cake mixture. Bake in pre-heated oven for 2 hours, then reduce heat to 300°F (150°C) Gas Mark 2, cover cake with a double thickness of non-stick bakewell paper and continue cooking for about 30 minutes, or until centre of cake is firm and springy. Test with a skewer to see if cake is done—it should come out clean.

When cooked, remove from oven and leave cake to cool in tin for 15 minutes, before turning out on to a wire rack. When cool brush top with a little warmed apricot jam or redcurrant jelly. Roll out remaining almond paste and cut an 8in (20cm) circle to fit top of cake. Level with a rolling pin, then make a criss-cross diamond pattern on almond paste using back of knife. Make a number of small balls from the odd pieces of almond paste left over and arrange them round top edge of cake, or divide almond paste into three pieces and roll each into a long sausage shape. Plait pieces together and arrange round edge of cake. Brush with beaten egg, sprinkle with caster sugar and put under a hot grill for a few minutes until a golden colour.

Decorate with a group of marzipan fruits made from left-over pieces of almond paste, or glacé and crystallised fruits. Tie a wide ribbon round the cake before serving. If you want to decorate this cake for Easter, make 12 balls from the remaining marzipan to represent the Apostles.

You can make your Simnel Cake well in advance as it keeps beautifully in an airtight tin.

EASTER

Easter is second only to Christmas in being one of the most celebrated of Christian festivals. It begins with Good Friday or God's Friday. On this day only really essential work was carried out, like feeding the livestock on the farms. After attending a service at church, most countrymen would spend the rest of the day sowing and planting in their gardens. Good Friday was the acknowledged time for planting potatoes, because the Devil was supposed to have no power over the soil that day.

The special association of Hot Cross Buns with Good Friday began only after the Reformation. Before this time it was customary to mark all dough with a cross before it went in the oven to ward off the evil spirits that might prevent it rising. The practice was abandoned as being 'popish' and retained only for that day in the Church's year when the symbol of the Cross had its greatest significance.

On Easter Eve boys and men called 'Pace Eggers' or 'Jolly Boys' used to tour surrounding towns and villages performing morality plays for gifts of money, fruit and hard-boiled eggs known as 'Pace Eggs'. These were dyed various colours, red being the favourite, with onion skins, furze flowers, birch bark and many other wild flowers and herbs. More elaborate effects were achieved by wrapping flowers and ferns round the egg before dyeing; do try this—you can get really beautiful results. Names and sentiments were printed on the eggs and given to friends and neighbours.

Easter Sunday may be any Sunday between 22 March and 25 April depending on the state of the moon. After the short break for Mothering Sunday, this was the first of the official holidays for the men and women in service at the big houses or on the farms. The previous six weeks' fasting was eased and a wide range of festive fare was eaten including many of our best-known recipes for small cakes —Shrewsbury, Tansy, Eccles, Banbury and many other pastry and mincemeat confections.

'Pace-Egg Rolling' was a custom carried out by children on Easter Monday. A steep grassy slope was chosen for this event and decorated hard-boiled pace-eggs were rolled down. The idea was to get your egg to roll as far as possible without cracking. Owners of cracked eggs had to forfeit them to owners of sound eggs, who promptly ate them! This custom was said to symbolise the rolling away of the stone from the tomb of Christ and is still observed in Lancashire.

I have started with a few traditional Good Friday recipes and continued with recipes for the long Easter weekend.

Good Friday Fish Pie (*serves 4–6*)
Fish Days were introduced in early medieval times with two objects in mind; one was 'to mortify the flesh by removing the immediate pleasure of meat-eating' and the second was 'to reduce carnal passions which were thought to be inflamed by too meaty a diet'! A very large number of days was involved during Lent, and all Fridays and Saturdays were kept as Fish Days until late in the Middle Ages. Wednesdays were likewise observed until the early fifteenth century. This meant that on about half the days of the year meat could not be eaten, but fish was prepared in equally magnificent dishes and certainly didn't 'mortify the flesh' of the rich! However, the poor *did* suffer as fresh fish was not widely available and they had to put up with the salted variety. It is hardly surprising that the Wednesday followed by the Saturday Fish Day fell into disuse, although Fridays and Lent were observed continuously until much later. There are still many people who like to eat fish on Good Friday.

Fish Pies were always a welcome part of Lenten fare. Originally they were filled with herrings, eels or salmon and dried fruit, covered with a strong paste. Later this was replaced with a richer, shorter pastry, which in its turn was dropped altogether, the fish being baked direct in an open dish covered with a layer of breadcrumbs. Herbs and anchovies replaced the dried fruit, and this was the forefather of our present-day Fish Pie.

78

This recipe uses a combination of smoked and fresh fish, which gives the pie a very good flavour and colour.

8 oz (225 g) smoked haddock fillet
12 oz (350 g) fresh haddock
½ pt (275 ml) milk
2 tablespoons water
1 bayleaf
1 oz (25 g) butter
1 small onion, chopped
1 oz (25 g) flour

2 oz (50 g) Cheddar cheese, grated
2 hard-boiled eggs, coarsely chopped
3 tablespoons fresh parsley, chopped
Freshly milled black pepper
Salt

FOR THE TOPPING:
1½ lb (675 g) freshly cooked potatoes
1 oz (25 g) butter

A little soured cream
Freshly grated nutmeg

Pre-set oven at 350°F (180°C) Gas Mark 4.

Put fish in ovenproof dish with milk, water and bayleaf. Bake uncovered in oven for 20 minutes. Remove and leave to cool a little. When it is cool enough to handle, skin and flake fish and set aside. Strain cooking liquid and reserve.

Melt butter in a saucepan and soften chopped onion without allowing it to brown. Stir in flour and cook for a few seconds. Add enough of the cooking liquor to make a creamy sauce, stirring continuously. Add grated cheese, flaked fish, eggs and parsley. Season with pepper. Taste, and add salt if necessary, but do be careful because some smoked haddock is very salty.

Put fish mixture into a 2 pt (1 l) pie dish. Next, cream the potatoes, with an electric hand whisk if you have one. Add butter and enough soured cream to make a smooth creamy mixture. Season and add some freshly grated nutmeg. Cover fish with mashed potato leaving rough peaks. Dot potato top with butter and sprinkle on more grated Cheddar cheese if you want. Bake near the top of the oven at 400°F (200°C) Gas Mark 6 for 25 minutes or until top is lightly browned and pie is bubbling round edges. Serve straight away.

Hot Cross Buns (*makes about 12*)
These buns were originally baked as one large one, but nowadays they are made individually. Traditionally they were eaten hot for breakfast on Good Friday as were Saffron Buns. In my family we have always eaten them hot with our morning cup of tea in bed— my father used to spoil us. It is an excellent start to the Easter celebrations. This particular recipe is full of fruit and spicy as a Hot Cross Bun should be.

$\frac{1}{2}$ pt (250 ml) milk and water mixed	2 oz (50 g) caster sugar
$\frac{3}{4}$ oz (22 g) fresh yeast	2 oz (50 g) butter
1 lb (450 g) plain flour	2 eggs, beaten
$\frac{1}{2}$ teaspoon salt	6 oz (175 g) currants, washed
$\frac{1}{2}$ teaspoon mixed spice	1 oz (25 g) candied peel, finely chopped (optional)
$\frac{1}{2}$ teaspoon ground cinnamon	4 oz (125 g) shortcrust pastry
$\frac{1}{2}$ teaspoon grated nutmeg	

TO FINISH:

2 oz (50 g) sugar — 2 tablespoons water

Warm milk and water mixture carefully to blood heat–98°F (37°C). Cream the fresh yeast with a little of this liquid. Leave in a warm place for 10 minutes or until frothy.

Sieve flour, salt and spices into a warm mixing bowl. Stir in caster sugar. Rub in butter with fingertips. Make a well in centre of flour, pour in frothy yeast mixture, remainder of liquid, beaten eggs, currants and candied peel (if you are using it). Using your hands, mix together until a soft dough is formed.

Turn dough on to a floured board and knead for about 10 minutes or until dough is elastic. Place it in a warmed, greased bowl. Sprinkle with extra flour and cover with a clean tea-towel. Set dough to rise in warm place for $1\frac{1}{2}$ hours, or until it has doubled in bulk, then knock down dough and leave to rise again for another 30 minutes.

Pre-set oven at 425°F (220°C) Gas Mark 7. Shape dough into small round buns and arrange on greased baking sheet. Leave to prove for about 15 minutes. Roll out shortcrust pastry on a lightly floured board and cut into strips to make crosses on each bun using a little water to stick on strips.

Bake in centre of pre-heated oven for 20 minutes or until browned on top. A steamy atmosphere in the oven is best for baking these buns, so place a roasting tin of boiling water at the bottom of oven while they are cooking. When ready, remove from the oven and leave to cool.

To finish the buns, put sugar and water into a heavy-based saucepan and heat gently until sugar has dissolved. Then increase heat and boil rapidly for a few minutes until a syrup has formed. Remove from heat and brush over your buns until all syrup is used. Store in polythene bags until wanted. These buns will freeze well.

Traditional Hot Cross Buns *(makes 12 buns)*
For a change and to be more traditional, why not bake one *large* bun. When you first mix your dough, roll out to a rectangle to fit a roasting tin about 12 x 9in (30 x 23cm). Brush inside of tin with

butter and put in dough. Mark into 12 squares with a sharp knife. Leave in warm place for 1½ hours until doubled in size. Make crosses with shortcrust pastry as before and mark each square. Bake as before.

Remove from oven and leave to cool for a few minutes, then cut into 12 squares. Transfer squares to a wire rack, and brush with syrup as before.

Lenten Leek Tart *(serves 6–8)*

In the past, leeks were specially raised for Lent, to bring some flavour into the Lenten fast. No meat was allowed, so vegetables with plenty of flavour were popular, cooked either on their own or with fish dishes. In this tart, eggs are included, but when fasting was very strict, they would not have been allowed.

8 oz (225 g) plain flour	1 egg yolk
Pinch of salt	1 tablespoon iced water
6 oz (175 g) butter	

FOR THE FILLING:

1½ lb (675 g) leeks	2 oz (50 g) Farmhouse Cheddar
Clove of garlic	cheese, grated
2 tablespoons olive oil	Salt
1 oz (25 g) butter	Freshly milled black pepper
2 eggs	Pinch of mace
4 fl oz (100 ml) double cream	

To make the pastry, sift flour and salt into a mixing bowl. Rub in butter. Mix egg yolk with water and add to flour. Mix with a fork then knead gently until a smooth paste is obtained. Roll into a ball, wrap in cling film or a polythene bag and leave in refrigerator for 1 hour.

When ready to bake tart, pre-set oven at 375°F (190°C) Gas Mark 5. Bring pastry to room temperature, then roll out thinly and use to line a buttered 9in (23cm) flan ring. Prick base with a fork and line with foil. Fill with dried beans and bake in pre-heated oven until almost cooked, about 15–20 minutes. Remove beans and foil and cool slightly before filling with the leek mixture.

Reduce the temperature to 350°F (180°C) Gas Mark 4. Roughly chop the cleaned leeks and garlic. Put olive oil and butter into a large pan, add leeks and garlic and cover with a lid. Cook slowly until softened. Meanwhile whisk together the eggs, cream and two thirds of cheese. Liquidise leeks with egg mixture. Taste and season well with salt, pepper and mace. Pour into prepared pastry case and top with remaining cheese. Bake in pre-heated oven for 15–20 minutes or until firm and golden in colour. Serve immediately.

Pease Pottage (*serves 6*)

White and grey pease pottage, or soup, was served during Lent in medieval days. It was usually flavoured with minced onion and sugar or honey and often coloured with saffron. However, I think this recipe using green peas, which is also very old, is much more to our taste now. The combination of lettuce and peas dates back to the seventeenth century.

4 oz (125 g) frozen or fresh peas
1½ pt (845 ml) chicken stock
1 oz (25 g) butter
1 medium onion, chopped
1 small rasher green bacon
  (optional)
¼ teaspoon ground mace
2 small sticks celery, chopped

1 oz (25 g) plain flour
½ teaspoon fresh rosemary leaves
Chopped mint to taste
¼ teaspoon ground cloves
Salt
Freshly milled black pepper
½ lettuce, shredded

FOR GARNISH:
4 rashers good-flavoured green bacon
Fresh mint leaves to cover bacon rashers
Tiny triangular sippets of white bread fried in butter

Cook peas in stock for a few minutes until just tender. Melt butter in a saucepan and fry chopped onion and bacon (if using), cut into strips, until pale golden colour. Add chopped celery, cover with lid and 'sweat' until soft and buttery. Stir in flour, rosemary leaves and spices. Add peas, stock and lettuce. Simmer for 10 minutes. Pass through a sieve, mouli or blender.

Make the garnish by de-rinding bacon and stretching rashers with back of a knife. Lay mint leaves on each and roll up tightly. Secure each roll with a cocktail stick and fry gently until bacon is cooked inside. Remove sticks and cut each roll into thin slices.

Reheat soup gently, check seasoning and add chopped mint to taste. Just before serving, add sippets of fried bread and sliced bacon rolls, and a swirl of cream.

Saffron Bread (*makes 1 loaf*)

This is the English pre-Reformation Lenten bread probably first made in the late fifteenth or early sixteenth century. Originally it was not a sweet bread, but later sugar, spices, rose water and currants were added. This sweet version makes a delicious tea-bread. The crust is shiny and golden and the inside a delightful yellow colour. It keeps well and is very good toasted and spread with butter.

Saffron bread was always eaten at Easter in the West Country, but is now baked and eaten all the year round.

Generous pinch of saffron strands	6 oz (175 g) currants
½ pt (250 ml) hot milk	2 oz (50 g) candied peel, chopped
½ oz (15 g) fresh yeast	½ teaspoon ground mace ⎫
3 oz (75 g) caster sugar	⎬ optional
1 lb (450 g) plain flour	1 teaspoon cinnamon ⎭
6 oz (175 g) butter	Clotted cream

Infuse saffron in hot water for at least 30 minutes, then strain and reheat the liquid until lukewarm. Cream yeast with 1 teaspoon of the sugar and gradually blend in the saffron milk.

Reserve 1 teaspoon of flour. Sieve the remainder into a bowl with the spices, if you are using them. Rub in butter, make a well in centre and pour in yeast liquid. Sprinkle reserved flour over surface of yeast liquid and allow to stand in a warm place for about 15 minutes until frothy. Add fruit and peel and remaining sugar. Mix to a soft dough. Cover and allow to rise in a warm place until double in size.

Pre-heat oven at 350°F (180°C) Gas Mark 4.

Turn dough out on a floured surface, knead lightly and shape to fit a greased 8in (20cm) round cake tin. Bake in pre-heated oven for about 1 hour until firm to the touch and golden brown on top. Leave to cool in tin. Serve fresh, in slices, spread with clotted cream.

Baking in this round shape is traditional, but you can bake in a loaf tin if you wish.

Saffron or Revel Buns (*makes 16*)
These are the original 'Hot Cross Buns' served hot for breakfast on Good Friday morning. They were also made for other annual revels especially in the West Country, where they are still extremely popular.

Generous pinch of saffron strands	4 oz (125 g) butter
¼ pt (150 ml) hot milk	¾ oz (22 g) fresh yeast
1 lb (450 g) plain flour	1 teaspoon caster sugar
Pinch of salt	4 oz (125 g) clotted cream
½ teaspoon ground cinnamon	2 eggs, beaten
	4 oz (125 g) currants, washed

FOR THE GLAZE:
Beaten egg	Caster sugar

Soak saffron in hot milk for 30 minutes.

Sift flour, salt, and spice into a bowl and rub in butter. Cream yeast with teaspoon of caster sugar. When lukewarm, strain saffron-flavoured milk and gradually blend into yeast mixture with cream and beaten eggs. Make a well in centre of dry ingredients and pour in yeast liquid. Add currants and mix to a soft dough. Turn out on a floured surface and knead for 3 minutes. Return to bowl, cover, and allow to stand in refrigerator overnight until double in size.

Pre-set oven next day at 375°F (190°C) Gas Mark 5. Shape dough into 16 round buns. Arrange on greased baking trays, cover and allow to prove in a warm place for about 15 minutes. Brush lightly with beaten egg, sprinkle with caster sugar and bake in pre-heated oven for about 15 minutes, until firm and golden brown. Cool on a wire rack, or serve immediately spread with plenty of butter.

Chocolate Easter Eggs

The custom of exchanging eggs at Easter is an ancient one. Eggs were considered to be symbols of fertility and new life. Nowadays we exchange chocolate eggs rather than hard-boiled and they are most rewarding to make and decorate. The most important thing is to use good quality chocolate, although some makes of cooking chocolate are easier to handle. You will also need metal or plastic moulds which are available in various sizes from good kitchen equipment shops.

Chocolate is a little temperamental, so melt it carefully. Break it into small pieces and place in a bowl over a saucepan of cold water. Make sure that the base of the bowl does not touch the water and that it is wedged into the pan, so that steam does not escape round the sides of the bowl. (Humidity will spoil the texture and gloss of your chocolate egg.) Heat the water gently, but don't allow it to boil. Remove the pan from the heat and stir the chocolate until it is completely melted. Half fill each mould with chocolate and tilt, to run the chocolate to the edge of the mould and coat it evenly all round. Repeat this two or three times, then pour surplus chocolate back into the basin. Run your finger round the edge of the mould to remove surplus chocolate then turn it, rounded side up, on a cool flat surface. As the chocolate shells cool, they shrink slightly and may be removed by pressing gently at one end. Don't handle the outer shell more than you have to, because your fingers will mark the shiny surface. The shells can be joined to make an egg by lightly touching the two halves on to a warm tin, so that just sufficient chocolate melts to enable them to set firmly together.

Decorate your Chocolate Eggs with crystallised primroses, violets and mimosa (see recipe below) and velvet ribbon; pipe on flowers or perhaps a child's name; or wrap in coloured tinfoil.

Crystallised Flowers

Flowers have been crystallised since the Middle Ages. They were added to salads, used to decorate puddings and sweets and served as sweetmeats at the end of a meal. A great variety of flowers can be preserved in this way, but if you are going to eat them you must be certain they are not poisonous. Avoid any flower which comes from a bulb as these are *not* edible. Some of the flowers which give very attractive results are violets, primroses, mimosa, roses (whole or individual petals), plum, apple, cherry and pear blossom, borage, individual hydrangea blossoms, marigolds, pansies, nasturtiums, carnations, sprigs of rosemary and mint leaves. Pick the flowers on a dry, sunny day when the dew has dried from them. The process is easy and extremely rewarding—I have become addicted!

Whole flowers or flower petals	Rosewater
1 oz (25 g) gum arabic	Caster sugar

Put gum arabic into a small bowl. Cover with a little rose water. Leave covered for 24 hours. (You can buy gum arabic from good chemists. If not available, use a lightly beaten egg white without rose water. This will not give such a good result, but is very acceptable.)

When the gum arabic has dissolved in the rosewater, carefully paint it over each flower petal using a fine paint brush. Make sure that the petals are completely coated on both sides, or they will not be properly preserved. Sprinkle all over with caster sugar, preferably from a sifter (you get an even coating with this). Place carefully on a sheet of greaseproof paper with a light covering of caster sugar or in a sieve. Dry in a warm place for 24 hours, until hard and crisp. Store on greaseproof paper in an airtight tin until wanted. Crystallised flowers will keep for several months without losing their colour.

Use to decorate fruit fools, creams, syllabubs, trifles and any other suitable puddings. Violets and primroses look delightful on an Easter Cake and make a change from Easter chicks and eggs!

Easter Biscuits *(makes about 18)*

These bright yellow curranty biscuits are a traditional treat for Easter Sunday. In the past, they would be eaten after church on Easter morning and children loved them so much they would carry on eating them for the rest of the day!

Currants have been customary fare on certain high days and holy days since the sixteenth century. Several reports have been found concerning individuals who found themselves without sufficient money to purchase currants on these special days and hanged themselves as a result!

6 oz (175 g) plain flour	4 oz (125 g) caster sugar
2 oz (50 g) rice flour	2 egg yolks
1 teaspoon mixed spice	3 oz (75 g) currants
4 oz (125 g) butter	1–2 tablespoons brandy or milk

TO FINISH:
1 egg white, lightly beaten	Caster sugar

Pre-set oven at 350°F (180°C) Gas Mark 4.

Sieve the two flours with the spice. Cream butter and sugar together until light and fluffy. Beat in egg yolks one at a time, then add currants. Work in flour mixture with enough brandy or milk to make a stiff paste. Turn out on a floured board and knead until smooth. Roll out to a thickness of about ¼in (½cm). Cut into 4in (10cm) rounds with a fluted cutter.

Place biscuits on greased baking trays. Brush with egg white and sprinkle with caster sugar. Bake in pre-heated oven for 15–20 minutes until pale golden and crisp. Remove when cooked and leave on the trays for 5 minutes. Transfer to a wire rack to cool completely. Store in an airtight tin until needed. The biscuits can be piped with a cross of glacé icing if you wish.

Ham Cooked in Cider

Bacon and ham were traditionally served at Easter. The ham was kept on one side through the Lenten fast and brought out again on Easter Sunday, and usually eaten with roast veal.

In this recipe, the ham is simmered in a mixture of water and cider or wine with a bunch of clean hay, herbs and vegetables and finished off in the oven to glaze. The practice of including a little hay goes back at least 200 years and is said to improve the flavour of the meat—it is still used in France. This recipe certainly tastes good, so maybe the hay *is* responsible!

10 lb (4·5 kg) ham	Large bunch of fresh herbs
1 pt (500 ml) dry cider or white wine	1 clove garlic
4 carrots, in large pieces	2 tablespoons brown sugar
2 large onions, stuck with cloves	2 bayleaves
Small bunch of sweet clean hay	12 peppercorns

Soak ham overnight in cold water, changing water if possible. Scrape rust from skin and pat fairly dry. Put into a large pan with cider or wine and enough water to cover. Add vegetables, and all other ingredients. Bring to boil and remove any scum which comes to the surface. Reduce heat and simmer gently for 3 hours. If you are cooking a smaller joint, simmer for 25 minutes per 1 lb (450 g). When ham is cooked, take out of stock, drain and peel off skin. Cut diamond shapes on fat and cover with your chosen glaze (see recipes with Christmas Baked Ham, pages 23–4). Bake in oven at 375°F (190°C) Gas Mark 5 for 30 minutes.

Serve hot or cold with Spiced Apple Sauce with Sherry (page 109) or Plum Sauce (page 88).

Marzipan Eggs (*makes about 24*)
These make very attractive presents to give at Easter especially when packed in small wicker baskets. They can also be used to decorate your Easter cake.

8 oz (225 g) ground almonds	1 teaspoon vanilla essence
8 oz (225 g) caster sugar	A little rose water
2 egg whites	

COLOURING FOR EGGS:
2 oz (50 g) caster sugar	Food colourings
1 egg white, whisked	

Mix together ground almonds and sugar. Whisk egg whites stiffly and add to mixture with vanilla essence and rose water. Mix to a stiff dough. Divide mixture and shape into little eggs.

I suggest you use 4 colours–say, green, blue, pink and yellow, for your eggs. Colour ½ oz (15 g) of sugar by adding a tiny drop of one of your chosen colours and stir until it is mixed thoroughly. Continue until you have your 4 coloured sugars. Dip each egg into the whisked egg white and then into the coloured sugars. This makes the eggs appear speckled and very pretty.

Dry on greaseproof paper for 24 hours, then store in airtight jars until you want to use them.

Roast Saddle of Lamb
Roast spring lamb is usually served for lunch on Easter Sunday. The lamb represents the innocence of Christ. Young animals such as kids, calves, and lambs have always been eaten at the Easter feast.

A saddle is the classic joint of lamb made up of the two loins together from ribs to tail, and can weigh up to 10 lb (4·5 kg). The kidneys are sometimes attached to the saddle and sometimes removed and tucked into the bone on top. They can be cooked with the joint, but it is really better to remove them as they do get rather over-cooked. Cook them separately and replace in joint before serving.

1 saddle of lamb	Freshly milled black pepper
2 cloves garlic	Little oil or dripping
6 sprigs of rosemary	Large glass of port or red wine
Salt	

Pre-set oven at 350°F (180°C) Gas Mark 4.

Place joint in a large roasting tin. Rub with garlic and make slits near bones. Put sprigs of rosemary and slivers of garlic in these slits. Season with salt and plenty of pepper. Brush all over with oil or dripping. Cook in a moderate oven for 25 minutes per 1 lb (450 g) and 25 minutes over. Baste saddle several times during cooking. Cook kidneys separately in oven.

When cooked, drain off all excess fat and add a large glass of port or red wine to pan juices. Season well and reduce on top of stove until it thickens slightly.

Serve lamb on a large platter (having replaced kidneys) decorated with fresh sprigs of rosemary and with redcurrant jelly or Plum Sauce (see recipe below). The saddle should be carved along the backbone.

Plum Sauce

This sauce is very good with Roast Lamb or Ham. Leave out the chopped fresh mint if you want to serve it with the latter.

1 lb (450 g) fresh red cooking plums (or 1 tin red plums)
½ pt (250 ml) white wine vinegar

4 oz (125 g) sugar
1 tablespoon fresh mint, chopped

Stew plums gently in vinegar with sugar for about 10 minutes or until soft. If you are using tinned plums, just heat them with the vinegar and sugar. (You may not need as much sugar.) When cooked, remove stones and stir in the mint. Serve hot.

This sauce freezes well, and will keep for a week in the refrigerator.

MIDSUMMER EVE

Midsummer Eve, 23 June, is also known as St John's Eve after John the Baptist, and is a time for sun worship. An old custom was to light bonfires after nightfall or at midnight. People would dance round these fires and when they burned less fiercely they would leap through them to bring good luck and protection from the evils of witchcraft. Fires are still lit on Midsummer Eve in the West Country.

The sowing of hempseed on Midsummer Eve used to be a popular means for a girl to find out who her future husband would be—he would appear behind her! Also the plant called St John's Wort was gathered and hung up near the door or window to act as a protection against evil spirits. Another old custom was for people to sit all night in the porch of their local church to see the spectres of those in the parish who would die that year knocking on the church door.

Besides being a religious festival, Midsummer Day or St John's Day is one of the quarter days in England when rents are due. The long, warm (hopefully) summer evenings are perfect for garden supper parties, so here are a few suitable recipes using summer fruits and produce.

Blackcurrant Sorbet (*serves 6–8*)
A sorbet is much lighter and more refreshing than ice-cream. You can use either the juice or flesh of most fruits and I have suggested some variations following this basic recipe.

1 lb (450 g) blackcurrants	¼ pt (150 ml) water
6 oz (175 g) sugar	

Cook blackcurrants for a few minutes in a heavy-based saucepan until juice begins to run—don't bother to top and tail them. Put fruit through a sieve or blender and cool. Heat sugar and water together until sugar dissolves and then bring to boil. Continue boiling for 5 minutes and cool. When cold, combine with fruit pulp and freeze. When ready to serve, scoop into glasses and decorate with crystallised mint leaves and a bunch of fresh blackcurrants.

Variations:
Cherry, Grape, Gooseberry or Redcurrant
Use exactly as foregoing recipe.

Loganberry or Raspberry
Use 8 oz (225 g) fruit, sprinkle with 2 oz (50 g) sugar and leave for
1 hour. Make a syrup with ¼ pt (150 ml) water and 6 oz (175 g)
sugar. Sieve fruit and mix resulting juice with sugar syrup and juice
of 1 lemon. Freeze.

Peach, Pear or Strawberry
Purée 4 large peaches, 2 large ripe pears or 8 oz (225 g) strawberries.
Make a sugar syrup with 6 oz (175 g) sugar and ¼ pt (150 ml) water
and cool. Stir in juice of 1 lemon (and 2 tablespoons Cointreau for
Strawberry Sorbet only). Combine fruit purée and syrup and freeze.

Burnt Orange Creams with Strawberries *(serves 8)*
This recipe is supposed to have originated in Scotland in Tudor
times. It is similar to the delicious French *crème brulée*. There are
endless variations on this creamy pudding, some with lemon rind
added, some vanilla or bay leaf. All are very rich and creamy. This
particular version is similar to the Trinity College Cambridge
Burnt Cream, which was a great favourite during May Week, but
orange has been added.

1 pt (500 ml) double cream	1 tablespoon orange rind,
2 in (5 cm) piece vanilla pod	grated
8 egg yolks	Soft light brown sugar
2 oz (50 g) caster sugar	1 lb (450 g) fresh strawberries
2 tablespoons orange liqueur	Clotted cream

Rinse a heavy saucepan with cold water and leave a film of cold
water on bottom. Pour in double cream and vanilla pod and heat to
just below simmering point over a low heat.

Meanwhile, beat egg yolks and sugar together until thick and
pale in colour. Slowly pour hot cream on to yolk and sugar mixture,
stirring slowly. Blend in orange liqueur and orange rind. Rinse out
saucepan and again leave a film of water on bottom. Pour in custard
mixture and cook over a very low heat stirring continuously with a
wooden spoon. Continue stirring until mixture thickens, but on no
account must it boil. Remove vanilla pod.

Sieve custard into individual china or pottery dishes and allow to
cool. Refrigerate for 5 or 6 hours or overnight.

An hour before you are ready to serve, pre-heat grill and sprinkle
an even layer, ¼in (½cm) thick, of soft brown sugar over top of
custard. Place individual dishes in a shallow roasting tin filled with
ice cubes and place under grill until sugar melts and caramelises.
(This takes only a few seconds so watch carefully.) Remove from
grill and allow to cool, but do not put in refrigerator or sugary top
will go soft. Serve with fresh strawberries and clotted cream.

Chilled Fish Cream (*serves 6*)

A dish similar to this would have adorned the Georgian table set for a summer meal, together with several other fish dishes such as fried eels and salmon cutlets. It is light and creamy and just right for a Midsummer supper, served with a crisp green salad.

8 oz (225 g) fish trimmings	4 oz (125 g) button mushrooms
Bunch of herbs	Squeeze of lemon juice
1 carrot, chopped	1 oz (25 g) butter
1 onion, sliced	½ pt (250 ml) double cream
2 tablespoons dry white wine	6 oz (175 g) fresh prawns, peeled
¾ pt (400 ml) water	1 tablespoon fresh tarragon,
Salt and pepper	parsley and chives, mixed
12 oz (350 g) haddock fillet	and chopped
½ oz (15 g) gelatine	

Put fish trimmings (you can ask your fishmonger for these), bunch of herbs (parsley, bayleaf and fennel), carrot, onion, white wine, water and seasoning in a saucepan. Simmer covered for 45 minutes. Strain resulting liquid and boil it fast, uncovered, for 10 minutes to reduce it. Now turn down heat to keep at slow simmer. Add fish and poach very gently for 10 minutes. Remove fish and allow to cool.

Melt gelatine in a cup with 2 or 3 tablespoons of hot fish stock, then stir into rest of stock and set aside to cool. Place in refrigerator until it is just starting to set.

Cut mushrooms into small dice and toss with a generous squeeze of lemon to keep them white. Melt butter in a small pan and fry mushrooms, without letting them brown, for 5 minutes. Whip cream to soft peaks. Flake cooked fish, stir in mushrooms and their liquid, and chopped prawns and herbs. Mix chilled stock lightly with fish mixture. Fold in whipped cream. Spoon mixture into a pretty china dish and chill until set.

Serve decorated with lemon and cucumber twists and sprigs of fresh parsley.

Chilled Lettuce and Pea Soup (*serves 6*)

The combination of lettuce and peas is a very ancient one. This recipe is good for using up your 'bolted' lettuces.

2 lettuces	8 oz (225 g) fresh or frozen peas
2 oz (50 g) butter	Salt
4 oz (125 g) onion, chopped	Freshly milled pepper
1 level tablespoon plain flour	¼ pt (150 ml) single cream
1½ pt (750 ml) milk	Sprigs of mint

Wash lettuces and chop roughly. Melt butter in a saucepan and add onion and lettuce. Cover and cook gently until soft. Stir in flour and cook for a further few seconds. Add milk gradually, stirring all the time. Bring to boil. Add peas, season well and simmer for about 20 minutes stirring occasionally. Cool slightly, then put through an electric blender or mouli. Pour into a chilled serving bowl and adjust seasoning. Chill well.

Serve with swirls of cream and garnished with mint sprigs.

Chranacan and Raspberries *(serves 6)*

Chranacan is a delicious luxury Scottish cream for eating on special occasions. It is made from toasted oatmeal and cream and is very good served with raspberries, blackberries or loganberries. Nowadays, it is often made with vanilla ice-cream instead of cream.

2 oz (50 g) coarse oatmeal	¼ teaspoon vanilla essence
¾ pt (400 ml) whipping or double cream	1 tablespoon caster sugar
2 teaspoons Scotch whisky	1 lb (450 g) raspberries

Spread oatmeal on a baking tray and toast in a moderate oven or under grill until edges are just starting to assume a brownish tinge. Allow to cool.

Beat cream until it stands in soft peaks and stir in whisky, vanilla essence, sugar and most of toasted oatmeal. Pile into a pretty dish and sprinkle with remaining oatmeal. Serve chilled with a bowl of raspberries or any soft fruit.

Fresh Peach Ice Cream *(serves 6)*

12 oz (350 g) fresh ripe peaches	Thinly pared rind 1 lemon
3 tablespoons lemon juice	¼ pt (150 ml) whipping cream
1 large can condensed milk	

Remove skins from peaches by dropping into boiling water for a few seconds. Cut into quarters, remove stones and soak in lemon juice. Roughly slice peaches and put into electric blender, add condensed milk, lemon rind and cream. Blend well until mixture is smooth. Pour into a shallow polythene container and freeze until firm.

About 30 minutes before you want to serve, remove from freezer. Leave to thaw a little in refrigerator so that flavour will emerge. Serve the ice cream plain or with a Chocolate Sauce (see page 33) and Almond Shortbread (page 60) or Langue de Chat Biscuits (page 94).

Fresh Raspberry Cheesecake *(serves 12)*

The cheesecake is not, as some people may imagine, a modern invention from America. It dates back to Georgian times and was made for special occasions. A Georgian cheesecake had a sweet pastry base and a lemon, almond, vanilla or rose water-flavoured cheese and egg centre. This recipe has a crumb base and a topping of fresh raspberries.

12 oz (350 g) digestive biscuits
10 oz (275 g) unsalted butter
1½ lb (675 g) cream cheese
8 oz (225 g) caster sugar
3 eggs
½ teaspoon orange flower water
1 lb (450 g) fresh raspberries
Redcurrant jelly
Whipped cream

Pre-set oven at 325°F (170°C) Gas Mark 3. Crush biscuits with a rolling pin. Melt 6 oz (175 g) butter and mix with crumbs. Press into 9in (23cm) loose-bottomed flan ring, covering bottom and sides. Chill in refrigerator while you make the filling.

Mix together cream cheese, sugar, eggs, orange flower water and remaining 4 oz (125 g) melted butter. Pour into crumb base. Bake in pre-heated oven on lowest shelf for 45–60 minutes. Keep an eye on cheesecake towards end of cooking time—it must not go brown or rise or it will taste tough and overcooked. Remove from oven and cool. Leave in a cool place overnight and serve following day.

To serve, remove from tin and top with fresh raspberries. Brush with melted redcurrant jelly and leave to cool. Pipe a lattice work of whipped cream across top of raspberries, and serve.

Gooseberry Fool (*serves 6*)
The real old-fashioned gooseberry fool was made with cream, or milk, and sugar rather than the more usual custard of modern times. It is a lovely summery pudding and very refreshing.

1 lb (450 g) green gooseberries
2 tablespoons water
6–8 oz (175–225 g) caster sugar
½ pt (250 ml) double cream

Top and tail gooseberries and put in a small saucepan with 2 tablespoons water and 2 tablespoons sugar. Cover with lid and stand in a roasting tin of water. Place over a low heat and allow to stew very gently for about 45 minutes until soft. Beat to a pulp with a wooden spoon, sweeten to taste and push through a mouli or sieve. Allow purée to cool. It should be fairly stiff and a pretty, soft green.

Whisk cream until it stands in peaks. Fold in gooseberry pulp leaving mixture looking slightly streaked rather than folded in smoothly—this looks much nicer. Put into your prettiest stemmed glasses and decorate with crystallised rose petals (see recipe on page 84) and small rosebuds or a few fresh gooseberries.

Serve chilled with Boudoir or Langue de Chat biscuits (see recipe on page 94).

93

Homemade Lemonade

Lemonade, using lemon juice, sugar and water, was a French invention. By the beginning of the eighteenth century it was being prepared and bottled with the addition of sulphur to preserve it. English drinkers were inclined to add an equal quantity of white wine to their lemonade! However, made with *water* it is an extremely refreshing drink on a hot summer's day.

TO MAKE SUGAR SYRUP:

8 oz (225 g) granulated sugar   1 pt (500 ml) water

TO MAKE LEMONADE:

2 tablespoons lemon juice per   Soda water or water
  glass   Sprigs fresh mint
Ice cubes   Fresh lemon slices

Put sugar and water in saucepan and dissolve sugar over a low heat stirring with a wooden spatula. Bring to boil and then leave to cool. Use this as base for lemonade.

When ready to serve, pour 3–4 tablespoons sugar syrup into each glass, and 2 tablespoons lemon juice. Add plenty of ice cubes and top up glass with soda water, if you want a fizzy drink, or water if a still drink is preferred. Decorate each glass with a sprig of mint and a slice of lemon. (Frost edge of glasses if you have time.)

Langue de Chat Biscuits *(makes 24)*

These are the perfect biscuits for serving with sorbets or fruit fools and are not difficult to make.

2 oz (50 g) butter   2 standard egg whites
2 oz (50 g) caster sugar   2 oz (50 g) plain flour
2–3 drops vanilla essence

Pre-heat the oven to 425°F (220°C) Gas Mark 7. Butter two baking sheets and dust them with a little flour. Shake off any excess flour.

Cream the butter, sugar and vanilla essence until the mixture is pale and fluffy. Put the egg whites into a bowl, but *do not* whisk them. Add them to the mixture a teaspoonful at a time, beating thoroughly after each addition. When the egg white has all been added, lightly fold in the sieved flour. Spoon the mixture into a piping bag fitted with a $\frac{1}{4}$in ($\frac{1}{2}$cm) plain nozzle, and pipe out in approximately 3in (7·5cm) lengths on to the prepared baking sheets. Leave plenty of space between each biscuit, because they spread out during cooking.

Bake them on a high shelf in the oven for about 8 minutes or until they are golden with brown edges. Leave them on the baking sheet for a few minutes, then cool on a wire tray. When cold, store in an airtight tin to keep them crisp until required. They are, however, at their best when just baked.

Lime Sorbet (*serves 6–8*)

You can buy fresh limes from most good greengrocers and they really are delicious in this sorbet. However, lemons, oranges or tangerines can be used in exactly the same way.

4 oz (125 g) sugar	4 fresh limes
¼ pt (150 ml) water	1 orange

Bring sugar and water to boil with a strip of lime rind added. After syrup has boiled for about 5 minutes, remove from heat and leave to cool. Finely grate rind and squeeze juice from limes and orange. Remove strip of lime rind from syrup and combine with fruit juice and grated rind. Mix well and freeze until half-set. Remove from freezer and beat well until light and frothy. Return to freezer. Remove 15 minutes before you want to serve. Serve in scoops in glass dishes. This is excellent served with scoops of Blackcurrant Sorbet (page 89) and Langue de Chat biscuits (page 94).

Marbled Rose Cream (*serves 4*)

You can make this delicate pudding with any soft fruit, but raspberries and strawberries are particularly suitable. The fruit can be slightly over-ripe without spoiling this recipe.

1 lb (450 g) raspberries or strawberries	½ pt (250 ml) double cream
6 oz (175 g) caster sugar	2 tablespoons rose water or kirsch

If you are using raspberries, put half of them into a saucepan, keeping several of the best on one side for decoration. Add half the sugar to pan and moisten with a tablespoon of water. Bring slowly to boil and simmer until raspberries start to yield their juice.

Push softened raspberries, pulp and juice through a sieve or mouli. Whisk cream until soft and thick, gradually adding remaining sugar. Mash all but a few reserved raspberries to a pulp and mix very thoroughly into cream with rose water or kirsch. Now add cooked raspberry pulp, stirring just enough to give a marbled effect.

Pour into your prettiest glass bowl and chill in refrigerator for at least 3 hours before serving. Decorate with the few remaining raspberries, dipped in beaten egg white and then in caster sugar, and a few crystallised mint leaves, or crystallised violets.

If you are using strawberries, don't cook them. Just chop up the berries and sprinkle with sugar. Leave for about 1 hour and proceed as with raspberries. Decorate with a few perfect berries.

Serve with Almond Shortbread (page 60) or Langue de Chat biscuits (page 94).

Midsummer Bowl (*serves 24*)

This is a delicious cooling drink ideal for serving at a Midsummer party. Serve chilled with plenty of crushed ice.

1 lb (450 g) fresh strawberries
2 oz (50 g) caster sugar
Juice of 2 large oranges
8 fl oz (225 ml) brandy
¼ pt (150 ml) Grand Marnier
¼ pt (150 ml) grenadine

2 bottles medium-sweet white
  wine, chilled
¾ pt (400 ml) soda water
2 small oranges, finely sliced
Ice cubes
Mint

Put hulled strawberries, sugar, strained orange juice, brandy and Grand Marnier into a large serving bowl or punch bowl. (You can use Cointreau or any orange-based liqueur instead of Grand Marnier.) Stir well, cover, and leave to stand for 1–2 hours.

Just before serving, add grenadine, chilled wine and soda water, and lots of ice cubes and mix. Float orange slices and sprigs of mint on surface. Serve in chilled glasses filled with crushed ice. (Put ice cubes in a polythene bag, wrap in a tea-towel and crush with a rolling pin.) If you want to make your drink look even more special, dip the rims of the glasses in water and then in caster sugar mixed with a few drops of orange food colouring.

Poached Fresh Salmon in White Wine

The season for fresh salmon is from February to August but it varies slightly, some rivers having an earlier season than others. Salmon is an expensive fish, but a whole fish costs slightly less per pound than fish bought by the piece and is very suitable for a large party. Allow 4–6 oz (125–175 g) per person, but remember when buying your fish to take the head into account (about one fifth of the total weight). Poach in a fish kettle or a large roasting tin covered with foil.

6–8 lb (2·8–3·6 kg) fresh salmon
2 carrots, sliced
2 onions stuck with a clove
½ pt (250 ml) white wine
Bouquet garni

12 peppercorns
2 bayleaves
Salt
2 slices of lemon

Clean your salmon, taking care to remove gills as well as insides. Run your thumb down backbone inside fish to remove dark membrane which lies against it. Wash salmon under cold running water. Don't remove head or tail, but snip away fins and trim tail into a sharp V-shape. Leave fish unscaled, because the scales will give extra protection during cooking and make the skin easier to remove afterwards. Dry your salmon thoroughly and wrap in a cloth dipped in oil or brush surface of fish with oil. Place gently in fish kettle and add all ingredients. Add enough water to cover fish completely and put on lid. Set kettle on lowest heat possible and bring to boil as slowly as possible. Immediately boiling point is reached, remove from heat and put to one side to cool completely in cooking liquor.

To dish up, carefully lift salmon out of kettle and drain on kitchen paper. Then peel off skin *very* carefully. Remove eyes with handle of a teaspoon and decorate fish with sliced cucumber, sliced hard-boiled egg, black olives and lots of parsley sprigs. Serve with home-made mayonnaise or hollandaise sauce, a cucumber salad and buttery new potatoes. You can really use your imagination in decorating your salmon with fancy shapes cut from cucumber skin, red pimentoes, olives and aubergine skin, and coating the fish with aspic. Enjoy your experimenting.

Redcurrants in Raspberry Juice (*serves 6*)

Strawberries are equally delicious in this recipe. They can be prepared in the same way and decorated with slices of lemon. The raspberry juice can also be served with poached peaches or pears, and Brandy or Peach Ice Cream (see recipes on pages 32 and 92).

1 lb (450 g) redcurrants	5 oz (150 g) caster sugar
8 oz (225 g) raspberries	

Wash currants and remove stalks. Place in a dish. Place raspberries in a small saucepan, heat gently, crushing fruit with back of a wooden spoon. When boiling, filter juice through a fine sieve, carefully squeezing pulp and pips. Add sugar to raspberry juice and pour over currants while still warm. Leave to stand in a cool place until you are ready to serve. Serve fruit in individual goblets with whipped cream.

Strawberries in Orange and Brandy (*serves 4*)

There is nothing more delicious than fresh strawberries chilled and served with a little orange juice poured over them—so simple, but so luxurious. You can also serve them with a little red wine or vermouth or kirsch.

1 lb (450 g) fresh strawberries	6–8 sugar lumps
1 large orange	2 fl oz (50 ml) brandy

Hull strawberries and place in a bowl. Rub lumps of sugar over rind of orange until soaked with oil from skin, then squeeze juice from orange. Crush sugar cubes and mix with orange juice and brandy. Pour syrup over strawberries, cover and chill thoroughly, 2 or 3 hours, before serving. Serve in glass dishes with whipped cream.

Strawberry Tart *(serves 6)*

4 oz (125 g) plain flour
2 oz (50 g) unsalted butter
2 oz (50 g) caster sugar
1 egg yolk
1 tablespoon cold water

2 drops vanilla essence
12 oz (350 g) fresh strawberries
8 oz (225 g) redcurrant jelly
Whipping cream to decorate

Sift flour into mixing bowl. Lightly rub in butter. Add sugar and mix in with your hands. Make a well in centre. Beat egg yolk with water and vanilla essence and pour into middle of well. Quickly work into a light paste. Chill in refrigerator for 1 hour.

Pre-set oven at 375°F (190°C) Gas Mark 5.

Put an 8in (20cm) flan ring on a buttered baking sheet. Butter inside of ring. Roll out prepared pastry and line flan ring. Line pastry with foil and fill with dried beans. Bake blind in centre of oven for 15 minutes. Remove beans, foil and ring and return pastry case to oven for a further 7–10 minutes to dry out. Cool case on a wire rack.

Make up tart just before you want to serve it, in order to keep pastry crisp. Arrange strawberries, points upwards, packed in tight circles in pastry case. Melt redcurrant jelly and coat each strawberry (using a teaspoon). Decorate with piped swirls of unsweetened whipped cream when redcurrant jelly is cold. Serve immediately with more whipped cream.

Summer Pudding *(serves 4–6)*

This is a marvellous way of serving summer fruits. It should be made the day before you need it, so that it has time to steep in its own juices. You can use strawberries, raspberries, redcurrants, gooseberries, cherries, loganberries, and blackcurrants. The best way is to use a combination of all these fruits, but not too many blackcurrants as these have a very strong flavour.

2 lb (900 g) mixed soft fruits
6 oz (175 g) sugar
White crustless bread
    preferably a milk loaf

2 tablespoons kirsch, vodka or
    gin
Single cream for serving

Cook fruits very gently with sugar until juice runs. (You may need more or less sugar depending on what fruit you have used.) Line a a 2 pt (1·1 l) pudding basin with slices of bread, cutting them to shape so that they all fit together neatly. Fill bread mould with fruit, juice and kirsch until tightly packed. Cover top completely with more trimmed slices of bread so that fruit is completely enclosed.

Cover with a plate that just fits top of basin and press it down with about a 2 lb (900 g) weight. Don't put on too heavy a weight or your pudding will collapse when you turn it out. Allow to stand overnight in a cool place.

Next day, remove weight and turn out carefully on to a serving plate. (Don't worry if pudding does collapse, because it will still taste very good!)

Serve well chilled with plenty of pouring cream.

Tennis Cake

No summer was complete without its tennis parties and teas in Edwardian days, and no tennis tea was without its Tennis Cake. Originally these cakes were round, but later they were baked in an oblong tin to represent a tennis court. They were covered with marzipan and pale green icing, and decorated with little silver tennis racquets and balls.

8 oz (225 g) butter	6 oz (175 g) currants
8 oz (225 g) caster sugar	6 oz (175 g) sultanas
Grated rind and juice of	2 oz (50 g) candied orange peel
½ orange	2 oz (50 g) glacé cherries
Grated rind of ½ lemon	1 oz (25 g) shredded blanched
4 eggs	almonds
2 oz (50 g) ground almonds	1 tablespoon milk to mix
10 oz (275 g) self-raising flour	

FOR DECORATION:
Green glacé icing   Silver balls
White glacé icing

Pre-set oven at 350°F (180°C) Gas Mark 4. Grease and line an oblong tin measuring about 8 x 12in (20 x 30cm). Cream butter and sugar with orange juice and rind and lemon rind until light and fluffy. Add eggs one at a time, beating well. (Add a little flour if mixture starts to curdle.) Stir in ground almonds and fold in flour, half at a time. Add fruit and shredded almonds. Mix to a dropping consistency with milk.

Put in prepared tin and bake in pre-heated oven for 1¼–1½ hours. Remove from tin and cool on a wire rack.

When cool, coat top and sides with green glacé icing. Pipe on white glacé icing to mark out tennis court and decorate with silver balls around edge of cake.

99

HARVEST HOME

Harvest celebrations vary from place to place depending on the crops. Nowadays they are usually held in August or September and take the form of thanksgiving services in the churches. Gifts of produce are taken to decorate the church and are later distributed to the sick and needy.

The Harvest Home Supper is still important in some rural areas. It used to be one of the few country feasts and took place in the farm's largest barn, celebrating the carrying home of the last harvest load or the cutting of the last upstanding corn. Often part of the corn was left standing to be cut ceremoniously and used to make a figure dressed in white and decorated with coloured ribbon. This figure was known as the Harvest Queen or Kern Doll. The villagers would come to rejoice with the farmer and his workers and there would be plenty of good food and drink and dancing to the music of pipe and fiddle. The men's hats were wreathed with flowers and everyone really enjoyed themselves.

Cider and Nut Cake
Serve in thick slices with cider or cider cup.

3 oz (75 g) butter
8 oz (225 g) self-raising flour
½ teaspoon mixed spice
Pinch of salt
3 oz (75 g) dark brown sugar
2 oz (50 g) stoned dates, chopped

2 oz (50 g) seedless raisins
2 oz (50 g) walnuts, chopped
2 tablespoons apple purée*
2 eggs, lightly beaten
2 tablespoons cider

FOR TOPPING:
1 oz (25 g) very dark brown
   sugar
1 oz (25 g) stoned dates, chopped

1 oz (25 g) walnuts, chopped
¼ teaspoon mixed spice

Grease and line tin about 9 x 5in (23 x 13cm). Pre-set oven at 350°F (180°C) Gas Mark 4.

Rub butter into sifted flour, spice and salt. Stir in sugar, dates, raisins and walnuts. Add apple purée, lightly beaten egg and cider. Put mixture into prepared tin. Mix topping ingredients together, and sprinkle over cake. Bake for 1¼ hours on middle shelf of pre-heated oven, or until evenly risen and springy. Turn out and cool on a wire rack.

This is a cake with a difference. The crunchy top makes a lovely contrast with the moist cake. (*A tin of stewed apple prepared for babies is ideal for this recipe.)

Curried Parsnip Soup (*serves 6*)

This is a lovely warming soup to serve at Harvest Home. There are plenty of good quality parsnips around at this time of year, so this soup is not expensive to make.

2 medium parsnips	2 pt (1·25 l) hot beef stock
3 oz (75 g) butter	Salt
4 oz (125 g) onion, chopped	Freshly milled black pepper
Large clove of garlic	¼ pt (150 ml) single cream
1 tablespoon flour	Fresh parsley or chives
1 heaped teaspoon curry powder	Sippets of fried bread

Peel and chop parsnip. Melt butter in a heavy-based saucepan, and add chopped parsnip, onion, and garlic. Cook gently for 10 minutes, covered with lid. Remove from heat and add flour and curry powder, blending in well. Cook for another 2 minutes, then stir in stock gradually until well mixed. Simmer gently with lid on until vege-tables are soft. Pass through an electric blender until smooth. Pour through a sieve (to remove any woody bits) into a clean pan, and season to taste with salt and pepper. Slowly reheat, then serve piping hot with the swirls of cream, a sprinkling of chopped parsley or chives, and a few sippets (cubes) of fried bread.

Harvest Apple Tart (*serves 8*)

Apple pie has been popular since medieval days. In Tudor and Stuart times candied orange peel, as well as cloves, cinnamon, rose water, dates and dried fruit, was added to the apples to give more flavour. Fresh lemon peel and lemon juice were added in Georgian times and often sliced quinces were mixed with the apple. It has long been part of festive fare, particularly when the apples were harvested. There are many recipes for apple pie, but this one is a little different, because it has a pastry base only and is therefore really a tart, and has rum and raisins added to the apple mixture.

8 oz (225 g) plain flour	1 egg yolk
Pinch of salt	2–3 tablespoons iced water
6 oz (175 g) butter	Few drops of rum
1 rounded dessertspoon caster sugar	

FOR THE FILLING:

3 oz (75 g) raisins
2 tablespoons rum
2 lb (900 g) cooking apples
3 oz (75 g) butter
8 oz (225 g) sugar

Grated rind of 1 lemon
½ teaspoon cinnamon
Vanilla pod
Beaten egg for glazing
Caster sugar for sprinkling

Start by making pastry. Sift flour and salt into a large bowl and rub in butter until mixture resembles breadcrumbs. Mix in caster sugar, then egg yolk mixed with 2 tablespoons iced water and a few drops of rum. Mix quickly, adding more iced water if necessary to make a firm dough. Wrap in cling film or put into a polythene bag and chill in refrigerator for at least 30 minutes.

Soak raisins in rum for at least 15 minutes. Peel, core and slice apples. Melt butter in a pan and add apples and sugar. Cook for a few minutes and then add lemon rind, cinnamon and vanilla pod, followed by rum and raisins. Cook carefully over a moderate heat, stirring continuously. Apples should form a slightly caramelised stewed mixture. Leave to cool.

Pre-set oven at 400°F (200°C) Gas Mark 6.

Remove pastry from refrigerator, bring to room temperature and roll out three-quarters of it to line an 8in (20cm) flan ring or dish. Fill case with apple mixture. Roll out remaining pastry and cut into ¼in (½cm) strips. Decorate top of tart with pastry strips to form a criss-cross pattern. Glaze pastry lattice work with beaten egg and sprinkle with caster sugar.

Bake in pre-heated oven for about 35 minutes or until golden brown. Lift out of tin and cool on a wire cooling tray.

Serve warm or cold with thick cream.

Harvest Cider Cup

Serve with hunks of Harvest Apple Tart (page 101) or Cider and Nut Cake (page 100). Make this cup 1–2 hours before serving.

2 pt (1·25 l) dry cider
¼ bottle orange squash
¼ bottle lemon squash
½ pt (250 ml) pineapple juice

½ glass medium sherry
Dash of Angostura bitters
Few strips cucumber rind
Orange and lemon slices

Place all ingredients in a large jug with lots of ice and slices of fresh orange and lemon. Add a bunch of crushed mint. Leave for at least 1 hour before serving.

Harvest Cider Syllabub (serves 4)

A seventeenth-century syllabub was usually made from cider and was standard fare for harvesters and other farm workers in late summer. It was more like a frothy drink than the 'set' syllabub eaten as a sweet in later times. However the recipe here is of the firm type, so that you can serve it as a dessert.

$\frac{1}{4}$ pt (150 ml) dry still cider
1 tablespoon brandy
Strips of peel from 1 lemon
2 oz (50 g) caster sugar

$\frac{1}{2}$ teaspoon grated nutmeg
$\frac{1}{2}$ pt (250 ml) double cream
Lemon juice to taste

Mix cider, brandy and lemon peel in a bowl and leave overnight. Next day, strain into a large basin. Stir in sugar and nutmeg. Trickle in cream slowly, stirring with a fork as you do so. Whisk until mixture is thick. Taste and whisk in a little lemon juice if you want. Spoon into small glasses and chill for several hours before use. Decorate with a little grated lemon rind and serve with Langue de Chat Biscuits (page 94).

Spiced Pear Pie (*serves 6*)
Pears were one of the first fruits to be grown in England and pear pie is mentioned in some Elizabethan recipes. It was part of traditional festive fare and appeared regularly at Harvest feasts.

8 oz (225 g) plain shortcrust pastry (made with 2 oz (50 g) margarine
    and 2 oz (50 g) lard)

$1\frac{1}{2}$ oz (40 g) granulated sugar
$1\frac{1}{2}$ oz (40 g) soft brown sugar
1 tablespoon plain flour
$\frac{1}{4}$ teaspoon grated nutmeg
$\frac{1}{4}$ teaspoon ground cinnamon
Grated rind of $\frac{1}{2}$ lemon

Grated rind and juice of
    1 orange
2 lb (900 g) cooking pears
2 oz (50 g) sultanas
1 tablespoon lemon juice
$1\frac{1}{2}$ oz (40 g) butter, melted

FOR GLAZING:
Milk
Granulated sugar

Pre-set oven at 400°F (200°C) Gas Mark 6.

Grease base of an 8in (20cm) round shallow pie dish. Divide prepared pastry in half. Roll out one half thinly and line pie dish. Prick all over base. Mix together sugars, flour and spices. Rub a little of mixture over pastry lining. Add grated orange and lemon rind to remaining mixture.

Peel, core and slice pears. Arrange in layers in pie dish, sprinkling each layer with sultanas, sugar and spice mixture, fruit juices and melted butter.

Roll out second piece of pastry to make a lid for pie. Damp edge of lining pastry, lift other piece on to top of pie. Press two edges firmly together, and knock up with back of a knife and flute edge. Make a few slits in top of pie to allow steam from fruit to escape. Brush lightly with milk and sprinkle with granulated sugar.

Bake in pre-heated oven for 20 minutes, and then lower heat to 375°F (190°C) Gas Mark 5, and continue baking for 25 minutes or until pie is cooked through. Serve hot or cold with cream.

Walnut and Honey Tart (*serves 8*)

Walnuts have been grown in this country for centuries and in the past were used in cooking far more than they are nowadays. Villagers used to gather them in the autumn and make them into pies, puddings, sauces, cakes, soups and stuffings. They were also added to meat and fish dishes, and pickled. If you are lucky enough to have a walnut tree in your garden, do look up some old recipes to get some new ideas. This tart is very, very rich, so a little goes a long way.

6 oz (175 g) shortcrust pastry (made from 2 oz (50 g) lard and 2 oz (50 g) margarine)

3 oz (75 g) butter	6 oz (175 g) clear honey
5 oz (150 g) soft brown sugar	½ teaspoon vanilla essence
Grated rind of 1 orange	4 oz (125 g) shelled walnuts
3 eggs, lightly beaten	in halves

Pre-set oven at 400°F (200°C) Gas Mark 6.

Roll out prepared pastry on a floured board and line an 8in (20cm) flan dish. Bake 'blind', by lining with foil, for 5–7 minutes. Remove from oven and take out foil. Set aside to cool.

Make filling by creaming butter in a bowl with wooden spoon or electric beater, gradually add sugar and orange rind and beat until well blended. Add beaten eggs and beat again. Then, add honey and vanilla essence mixing to a smooth consistency.

Sprinkle walnut halves in bottom of pastry case, pour over honey mixture (don't worry if it seems a bit runny, as it will set), and bake in pre-heated oven for 45 minutes or until set. It might take a little longer, but make sure it doesn't brown too quickly. If it does, reduce heat.

Serve cold with lots of whipped cream.

MICHAELMAS

This festival is also known as St Michael's Day and is held on 29 September. St Michael is one of the three archangels, the other two being St Gabriel and St Raphael, and was the object of a cult from the earliest Christian times—a church was built to him near Constantinople as early as the fourth century.

Michaelmas is one of the quarter days in England when the landlord used to hold his annual rent audit and provided a feast at the 'big house' for all his tenants. This day was also the date for the termination of the year of service for the men and women hired at the 'hiring fairs' held the previous year, who were for some reason anxious to change their master.

Popular fare for the Michaelmas feast was hot roast goose. This was the time of year when geese were in their prime, having just been fattened on gleanings from the wheat and barley harvest. Many Goose Fairs were held all over England, so called because of the large numbers of geese that were sold there prior to Michaelmas. Some still exist, but without the geese! On many country estates today, the landlord still provides a Michaelmas feast for his tenants, but it is now more likely to be held at the local pub and certainly won't consist of roast goose.

It is said that on Michaelmas Day the Devil puts his feet on all the blackberries, and it is considered unlucky to eat them after this; so eat your fill before 29 September.

Michaelmas Roast Goose (serves 8)

> 'Whoso eats goose on Michaelmas Day
> Shall never lack money his debts to pay.'

Long before the turkey was introduced in the sixteenth century, the goose was traditionally the festive bird of Britain. Serve it at Christmas for a change instead of roast turkey. Geese are still luxuries and quite rightly so; they are exceedingly rich and delicious, but provide a very small amount of meat for their size. In the past, to make the goose go further, a whole or jointed rabbit as well as sage and onion stuffing was put inside and this was given to the children as it was more easily digested.

Mature geese weigh 10–14 lb (4·5–6 kg) and a 10 lb (4–5 kg) bird should serve 8 people. As roast goose is rich and fatty, it is a good idea to accompany it with something plain and refreshing, such as red cabbage, a few rosy baked apples or a gooseberry or apple sauce.

1 x 10 lb (4·5 kg) young goose	Freshly milled black pepper
Prepared chosen stuffing	A little plain flour
Salt	

Pre-set oven at 400°F (200°C) Gas Mark 6.

Prepare your chosen stuffing (see following recipes). Stuff mixture into cavity of goose and sew up both openings with trussing string. Secure with skewers if necessary. Place goose on a wire rack in a roasting tin, prick all fleshy parts with a fine skewer or cocktail stick several times, season well with salt and pepper, and dust all over with flour.

Roast in pre-heated oven for 30 minutes to brown skin, then cover bird with foil or greaseproof paper, reduce heat to 350°F (180°C) Gas Mark 4, and roast for a further 2½–3 hours or until juices run clear when goose is pierced with a skewer. Baste and turn bird frequently during cooking, and pour off excess fat two or three times. (Goose fat is delicious for frying—particularly fried bread!)

Remove foil and greaseproof paper, baste again and turn oven up to 450°F (230°C) Gas Mark 8 for the last 10 minutes of cooking time to give skin a final crisping.

While goose is cooking, make stock by simmering giblets, with an onion, carrot, stick of celery, a bayleaf and peppercorns in 1½ pt (750 ml) water for 1–1½ hours. Use to make gravy.

To serve your goose, lift on to a warmed meat platter and make gravy from juices in roasting tin (remove all fat) and giblet stock. Serve with crisp roast potatoes, or Casserole of Potatoes and Onions (page 110), and Braised Red Cabbage (see page 111), and accompanied by Spiced Apple Sauce with Sherry or Gooseberry Sauce (see recipes on pages 109 and 108). Fried apple or pineapple make a good garnish, with watercress or fresh parsley.

Apple, Onion and Sage Stuffing
This stuffing is good with goose or pork.

1 medium-sized cooking apple	1 egg, beaten
1 small onion, chopped	Salt
4 fresh sage leaves, chopped	Freshly milled black pepper
4 pickled walnuts, quartered (optional)	Grated rind and juice of ½ lemon
4 oz (125 g) fresh white breadcrumbs	

Peel and grate apple into a bowl. Combine with all other ingredients and mix well. Stand for 1 hour in a cool place and then use to stuff cavity of goose or roll into small balls with floured hands and fry in very hot fat or dripping until golden brown and crisp. Drain on kitchen paper and serve around roast goose.

Liver and Olive Stuffing
This stuffing is suitable for duckling and game as well as goose. Use the liver of whichever bird you are stuffing.

8 oz (225 g) pork sausagemeat
2 oz (50 g) fresh white
   breadcrumbs
$\frac{1}{2}$ oz (15 g) butter
Liver, chopped
12 green olives, stoned and
   chopped

2 cloves garlic, chopped finely
1 tablespoon chopped fresh
   basil or 2 teaspoons dried basil
Salt
Freshly milled black pepper
1 egg, beaten

Lightly fry chopped goose liver in butter. Mix all ingredients together in a bowl. Season well and bind to a loose stuffing with beaten egg. Spoon into goose cavity.

Madam Sauce
This was served with the medieval goose and is not really a sauce. After the goose was cooked, it was cut apart and the forcemeat removed and combined with wine and spices to form a sauce that was poured over the pieces of goose.

$\frac{1}{2}$ teaspoon fresh sage, chopped
1 teaspoon parsley, chopped
$\frac{1}{2}$ teaspoon savory, chopped
4 tablespoons quince jelly
$\frac{1}{4}$ teaspoon ground ginger
$\frac{1}{2}$ teaspoon freshly grated
   nutmeg

2–3 fresh pears, chopped
1 clove garlic, crushed
3 oz (75 g) grapes, peeled and
   de-seeded
Salt
Freshly milled black pepper
$\frac{1}{2}$ teaspoon ground cinnamon

Mix all ingredients together in a bowl and season to taste. Spoon into cavity of goose.

Prune and Apple Stuffing
This is a good stuffing for goose or pork.

1 oz (25 g) butter
1 large onion, chopped
1 large cooking apple, chopped
$\frac{1}{2}$ teaspoon dried rosemary
A little brown sugar

12 large prunes, soaked
   overnight
Salt
Freshly milled black pepper

Melt butter and fry onion very gently until softened. Toss apple with this for a few minutes. Put in a bowl with herbs, sugar and chopped prunes. Mix into a loose stuffing, season to taste and spoon into cavity of goose.

Sage and Onion Stuffing

This is the traditional stuffing for Michaelmas Roast Goose, but do try the alternatives in this section for a change. If you want to stuff your goose with one of the other stuffings, make this recipe into small balls, coat in flour and shallow fry until crisp. Serve arranged around the goose. Also good with Roast Pork.

2 oz (50 g) butter
1 lb (450 g) onions, finely
  chopped
12 oz (350 g) fresh white
  breadcrumbs

1 egg, beaten
3 tablespoons dried sage
3–4 tablespoons single cream
Salt
Freshly milled black pepper

Melt butter in a pan and add onions. Cook gently until golden brown. Transfer to a bowl and stir in the breadcrumbs, egg and sage. Mix well, adding enough cream to hold the mixture together. Season to taste with salt and pepper.

Sausagemeat and Apple Stuffing

2 oz (50 g) butter, melted
2 medium-sized onions, chopped
Liver from goose, finely
  chopped
8 oz (225 g) pork sausagemeat

2 large cooking apples
6 oz (175 g) fresh brown
  breadcrumbs
Salt
Freshly milled pepper

Cook chopped onions gently in melted butter until golden. Add chopped liver and sausagemeat and cook until browned, breaking it up and stirring continuously. Peel, core and chop apples and add to pan. Continue cooking for 5 minutes, then transfer to a bowl and stir in breadcrumbs. Season and mix well. Spoon into cavity of goose.

Green Gooseberry Sauce

This makes a good alternative to apple sauce for serving with the Christmas or Michaelmas goose. It also goes very well with duck. In this particular old recipe, elder blossom and lemon are included to add extra flavour. If you can remember to make your gooseberry sauce when the elder flower is blooming and freeze it, so much the better, but don't worry if you forget—your sauce will still taste good!

10 oz (275 g) fresh green	1 teaspoon caster sugar
gooseberries	Salt
Finely grated rind and juice of	Freshly ground white pepper
1 lemon	½ oz (15 g) butter
2 sprigs young elder flower,	
if available	

Top, tail and wash gooseberries. Put in a pan with juice and rind of lemon and elder flower if available. Cover with tight-fitting lid, and without adding any more water to gooseberries than is already clinging to them after washing, toss pan over low heat until juices run. Poach fruit until tender. Put through a sieve to make a purée. Season with sugar, salt and pepper. Add knob of butter and stir in. This sauce has a tangy flavour. If you like it sweeter, add more caster sugar—this will depend a lot on the sweetness of your gooseberries. If your sauce is not a very good colour add a few drops of green food colouring. Serve sauce hot or cold.

Prune and Apple Sauce (serves 6–8)
Serve with goose or roast pork. It makes a change from apple sauce.

8 oz (225 g) dried prunes	1 tablespoon goose fat
½ pt (250 ml) dry cider	¼ teaspoon powdered cloves
8 oz (225 g) cooking apples	2 pinches powdered mace
½ medium onion, chopped	2 level tablespoons caster sugar

Soak prunes overnight in dry cider. Next day, place in a saucepan with ¼ pt (150 ml) of soaking liquor. Simmer until they are plump and tender. Press through a sieve or mouli, removing the stones.

Peel, core and chop apples. Soften chopped onion in a saucepan with tablespoon goose fat. Stir in chopped apples and simmer until a soft pulp. Stir in sieved prune mixture, spices and sugar. Taste and add more sugar and spices if necessary.

Reheat gently just before serving up the roast goose.

Spiced Apple Sauce with Sherry (serves 6–8)
This sauce can be made from cooking or hard eating apples depending on which you prefer. The addition of sherry makes it particularly festive. Serve with Michaelmas Roast Goose or Roast Pork.

1 lb (450 g) cooking or	¼ teaspoon grated nutmeg
eating apples	A little grated lemon rind
4 oz (125 g) caster sugar	1 oz (25 g) unsalted butter
1 tablespoon water	Sherry to taste
¼ teaspoon cinnamon	

Wash, peel, core and slice apples. Poach in a medium-sized saucepan with sugar, water, spices and lemon rind, until tender, stirring occasionally. Pass through a sieve or blender. Stir in unsalted butter and sherry to taste.

Serve sauce hot or cold, but make sure if you are serving it cold, that it really is well chilled.

Variations:
Add 1 oz (25 g) chopped walnuts to above recipe.
Add 1 oz (25 g) raisins and 1 pinch of dried sage to above recipe.

Baked Apples stuffed with Apricots (*serves 6*)
These apples make a very good accompaniment to Honey and Mustard Roast Pork and the Christmas or Michaelmas Roast Goose.

6 medium cooking apples	1 oz (25 g) butter
3 tablespoons soft brown sugar	2 tablespoons dried apricot
Grated rind and juice of	purée or homemade apricot
1 large lemon	jam

Pre-set oven at 375°F (190°C) Gas Mark 5.

Wipe apples and core them well. With a peeler, pare off about ½in (1cm) of the peel from top of each apple. Mix together sugar, lemon juice, rind and butter and pack this into apple cavities. Set apples in a baking dish and pour in just enough hot water to cover bottom, then bake whole until tender—about 25–30 minutes, depending on size.

Cool slightly, then carefully scoop out about 1 tablespoon or more of soft apple, taking care not to break skins. Put this pulp into a bowl and taste, adding a little more sugar and lemon juice if necessary. Add apricot purée. Fill apples with this mixture and reheat. Serve hot with your choice of roast meat, or as a pudding with lots of clotted cream.

Casserole of Potatoes and Onions (*serves 6*)
Potatoes cooked in this way are ideal to serve with your Michaelmas Roast Goose, because they are not as rich as roast potatoes. If you are planning to serve them with other roasts, grills, or steaks replace the stock with a mixture of double cream and milk, and sprinkle grated cheese over before cooking.

2 lb (900 g) potatoes	Salt
1 clove garlic, crushed	Freshly milled black pepper
2 oz (50 g) butter	Grated nutmeg
1 large onion, finely sliced	½ pt (250 ml) hot stock

Peel potatoes and slice very thinly. Put in large bowl of cold water and leave to soak to remove some of the starch.

Pre-set oven at 400°F (200°C) Gas Mark 6. Rub a large shallow baking dish with crushed garlic and 1 oz (25 g) butter. Drain potato slices and pat dry. Now, arrange a layer of potatoes over base of dish followed by a thin layer of finely sliced onion and a seasoning of salt, pepper and grated nutmeg. Continue with another layer of potatoes etc until everything is used up. Finish with a layer of potatoes and season.

Bring stock to boil and pour over potatoes. Dot remaining 1 oz (25 g) butter over surface. Bake in centre of oven for 1–1½ hours or until potatoes feel soft when tested with a knife and top is golden brown. Serve hot and decorated with fresh chopped parsley.

Spiced Braised Red Cabbage (serves 8)

Traditionally red cabbage has been served with roast goose. This recipe includes apples and is delicious. You will find, however, that you will not need to serve apple sauce as well—so try gooseberry for a change.

2 lb (900 g) red cabbage	¼ whole nutmeg, freshly grated
Salt	¼ level teaspoon ground
Freshly milled black pepper	cinnamon
1 lb (450 g) onions, chopped	¼ level teaspoon ground cloves
1 lb (450 g) cooking apples,	3 tablespoons brown sugar
chopped	3 tablespoons wine vinegar
1 clove garlic, chopped finely	½ oz (15 g) butter

Pre-set oven at 300°F (160°C) Gas Mark 2.

Cut cabbage very finely. In a large casserole, arrange a layer of shredded cabbage and season with salt and pepper. Cover with a layer of chopped onion and then a layer of chopped apple with a sprinkling of garlic, spices and sugar. Continue with these layers until everything is used up.

Next, pour in wine vinegar—red or white, it doesn't matter which—add knob of butter, put a tight-fitting lid on casserole and let it cook very slowly in oven for 2½–3 hours, stirring occasionally during cooking.

This dish can be cooked in advance and reheated if you want to save time—it will not spoil. It can also be cooked on the top of the stove if you wish.

Pears in Red Wine (serves 8)

Pears have been baked in red wine for centuries. Any firm pears can be used for this dish, and they can be served hot or cold. If you want to be more extravagant you can use port or sherry instead of red wine!

1 pt (500 ml) burgundy-type wine
8 oz (225 g) caster sugar
6 whole cloves
2 in (5 cm) cinnamon stick
Grated rind of 1 orange

Grated rind of ½ lemon
8 good-sized firm pears
Lemon juice
A little cochineal if necessary
Flaked, toasted almonds
Cream

Pre-set oven at 400°F (200°C) Gas Mark 6.

Make a syrup from wine, sugar, cloves, cinnamon and grated orange and lemon rind, by slowly dissolving sugar and then bringing up to boil. Simmer for 5 minutes.

Peel pears leaving stalks on. Drop into water acidulated with lemon juice to prevent them discolouring. Select an ovenproof dish just large enough to hold the pears sitting upright without tipping over. Pour over boiling wine syrup. Cover dish tightly with lid and bake until pears are tender, about 40 minutes.

With a slotted spoon, transfer pears to a warmed serving dish. Boil syrup down to a coating consistency. If colour is not bright enough add a very few drops of cochineal. Spoon hot syrup over pears until they gleam. Serve hot or cold sprinkled with toasted almonds and with lightly whipped and chilled cream to which a little pear brandy has been added.

Warden Pears (*serves 4*)
The old Bedford Fair once held at Michaelmas was famous for its baked pears. These were served from large earthenware pots into saucers and were known as 'wardens'. An old street cry was:

> Smoking hot, piping hot,
> Who knows what I've got
> In my pot? Hot baked wardens.
> All hot! All hot! All hot!

Warden pears may have been named after the Bedfordshire town of Wardon or after Walden Abbey, where pears were successfully cultivated by the Cistercian monks. These baked pears were sold in the streets of England, particularly in winter, until the 1860s. Pears, along with apples, were the first fruit trees grown in England, dating from the Middle Ages.

¼ pt (150 ml) strong still cider
½ teaspoon grated nutmeg
2 oz (50 g) soft brown sugar
2 oz (50 g) butter
4 firm ripe dessert pears

2 oz (50 g) desiccated coconut
Grated rind of 1 orange
2 tablespoons Cointreau (optional)
Cream

Pre-set oven at 325°F (170°C) Gas Mark 3.

Put cider in a saucepan with nutmeg, sugar and 1 oz (25 g) butter. Heat gently until sugar has dissolved and butter melted. Bring to boil and boil for 2 minutes. Peel, halve and core pears, and place in a shallow oven-proof dish, rounded side uppermost. Pour cider liquor over pears, cover and cook in moderate oven for about 40 minutes or until pears are just tender. (A few sultanas, seedless raisins or chopped dates can be added to pears before cooking if you want.)

Meanwhile, melt remaining 1 oz (25 g) butter in small frying-pan, add coconut with finely grated rind of orange and fry gently until golden brown, turning occasionally. Spoon out on to heatproof plate and leave to cool.

Just before serving, stir Cointreau into pears and sprinkle with fried coconut topping. Serve hot with lightly whipped or clotted cream.

HALLOWE'EN

Also known as All Hallow's Eve, this festival takes place on 31 October, and is a time when old superstitions are revived. This was the night that the spirits of the dead were supposed to appear. In certain parts of the country the custom was to light ceremonial fires for the relief of souls in hell. It was also thought to be a favourite night for witches to make their appearance, and country folk, being very superstitious, would take every precaution to safeguard themselves and their animals from the evil influences of witches and witchcraft.

All Saints' Day (1 November) and All Souls' Day (2 November) follow and the celebrations had much in common. Festival fires were lit, church bells rung, and prayers for the dead were chanted. Children and adults would go 'a-souling' and beg for soul-cakes or any other gift.

Nowadays, these three festivals are celebrated in one, on Hallowe'en, and this is more popular in Scotland and the North of England than in the South. Such games as ducking for apples and burning nuts are played. Lanterns are made out of pumpkins and turnips and people dress up as witches. Hot spicy drinks are served, also warming mugs of soup, large slices of chocolate cake and gingerbread and pumpkin pie. It is said that if you eat an apple at midnight on Hallowe'en, you won't catch a cold for twelve months. It hasn't worked for me.

Cloutie Dumpling (*serves 6–8*)

This is a spicy fruit pudding boiled in a cloth. In some parts of Scotland it is made for Hallowe'en when charms are put into it, as in a traditional Christmas Plum Pudding. Any dumpling left over can be cut into slices and fried with bacon for breakfast the next morning.

12 oz (350 g) self-raising flour, sieved
6 oz (175 g) shredded butcher's beef suet
4 oz (125 g) currants
4 oz (125 g) sultanas
4 oz (125 g) stoned raisins
½ apple, grated
1 rounded teaspoon cinnamon

1 rounded teaspoon ground ginger
1 rounded teaspoon mixed spice
5 oz (150 g) soft brown sugar
½ teaspoon bicarbonate of soda
½ teaspoon cream of tartar
1 egg, beaten
3 tablespoons black treacle
About ¼ pt (150 ml) milk to mix

Mix flour, suet, dried fruit, apple, spices, sugar and raising agents together. Mix egg with treacle and add to mixture with just enough milk to make a soft dough. Turn into a scalded, floured cloth and tie up, leaving room for dumpling to swell.

Plunge dumpling into a large pan of boiling water and give it 3 hours' steady boiling. Replenish with boiling water as needed. Turn pudding out on to a hot dish, removing cloth, and put it in the oven at 350°F (180°C) Gas Mark 4 for 10 minutes. This will dry the dumpling off and glaze the top.

Serve hot with sugar, home-made custard or a hard sauce such as Brandy or Rum Butter (see recipes on pages 41 and 42).

Curried Apple Soup (*serves 6*)

Although this is a fruit soup it is quite savoury, and I think you will enjoy its spicy flavour. Fruit has been made into soup or pottage since Elizabethan days, so I think it would be exciting to serve this recipe on All Hallow's Eve.

1½ oz (40 g) butter
1 medium-sized onion, chopped
1 carrot, chopped
1 stick of celery, chopped
2 level teaspoons mild curry powder
1 level teaspoon turmeric
1 level tablespoon flour
2 teaspoons tomato purée

2 pt (1·25 l) chicken stock
2 cloves garlic, crushed
2 bay leaves
¼ teaspoon thyme
¼ teaspoon oregano
2 large cooking apples
Salt
Freshly milled black pepper
Redcurrant jelly, if necessary

FOR GARNISH:
Chopped dessert apples

Soured cream

Melt butter in a large saucepan and add chopped vegetables. Sweat for 10 minutes with greaseproof paper over vegetables, and a lid on the saucepan, until vegetables are nice and buttery and softened but not browned. Stir in curry powder, turmeric, flour and tomato purée. Cook over a gentle heat for a few minutes. Gradually add cold chicken stock stirring continuously until blended. Add crushed garlic, bay leaves and herbs. Cook gently for about 30 minutes.

Meanwhile, wash apples, core and slice (don't bother to peel them). Add to soup, remove bay leaves and liquidise until smooth, or pass through a sieve or mouli. Return to a clean pan and bring slowly to the boil. Add salt and pepper to taste. Sweeten with a little redcurrant jelly if necessary. Lemon juice may be added if the soup lacks bite.

Serve piping hot in earthenware bowls, garnished with finely chopped green dessert apples and a swirl of soured cream.

Devils on Horseback *(serves 6)*

12 rashers streaky bacon
12 dried prunes, soaked overnight

2 slices fried bread or toast
Watercress to garnish

Stretch bacon rashers with back of a knife. Half cook under grill, and roll each rasher round a prune. Fasten with a fine skewer or cocktail stick and grill for 4–5 minutes or bake in a hot oven (400°F (200°C) Gas Mark 6 for 5–6 minutes.

Serve on a piece of fried bread or hot buttered toast and garnish with watercress.

Gingerbread Husbands *(makes about 18)*

On All Hallow's Eve or Hallowe'en the young maids of the villages had to eat a Gingerbread Husband to ensure that they would find a real husband! Gingerbread was often shaped into dolls for feasts and revels. There was always a gingerbread stall at fairs selling 'fairings' or gingerbreads.

1 lb (450 g) plain flour
1 dessertspoon ground ginger
½ dessertspoon cinnamon
Pinch of salt
4 oz (125 g) butter

4 tablespoons black treacle
8 oz (225 g) soft brown sugar
1 teaspoon bicarbonate of soda
1 tablespoon milk
A few currants to decorate

Sift flour with spices and salt into a large mixing bowl. Warm butter, treacle and sugar, until sugar dissolves and treacle melts, stirring continuously. Let this cool a little before stirring into flour mixture. Dissolve bicarbonate of soda in milk and add this to mixture to make a pastry-like dough. (You may need a little more milk.) Chill in refrigerator for about 40 minutes.

Meanwhile, make a cardboard pattern of your ideal husband!

Pre-set oven at 325°F (170°C) Gas Mark 3. Roll out your ginger-bread dough on a floured board. Cut it into Gingerbread Husbands, by using your cardboard template and cutting round it with a sharp knife.

Place your Husbands on a greased baking tray. Put currants on them for eyes, noses, and buttons. Bake them for about 15 minutes or until evenly brown. Cool on a wire rack. Store in an airtight tin.

Hallowe'en Devil's Cake

This is an American cake, taken there by early settlers, and it has become established over the years as a traditional favourite for Hallowe'en. You can decorate it with a large spider's web piped on in white glacé icing.

3 oz (75 g) plain chocolate
3 tablespoons warm water
6 oz (175 g) butter
10 oz (275 g) soft dark brown
   sugar

1 teaspoon vanilla essence
3 eggs, beaten
6 fl oz (150 ml) milk, soured
   by adding juice of ½ lemon
10 oz (275 g) self-raising flour

FOR SYRUP AND FILLING:
2 tablespoons black treacle
1 teaspoon ground cinnamon
1 tablespoon cocoa powder

2 tablespoons dark rum or
   sherry
Apricot jam to fill

FOR FROSTING:
1 lb (450 g) granulated sugar
½ pt (250 ml) water
1 tablespoon golden syrup

2 oz (50 g) unsalted butter
2 oz (50 g) cocoa

Pre-set oven at 350°F (180°C) Gas Mark 4. Prepare two 8in (20cm) sandwich tins by greasing and lining with discs of greased grease-proof paper.

To make the cake, first break chocolate into small pieces and put in a bowl over a pan of very hot water. Add warm water and dissolve chocolate stirring until smooth. Remove from heat and cool slightly.

Cream butter with sugar and vanilla essence. Beat in eggs and melted chocolate. Add soured milk alternately with sieved flour. Bake just above centre of oven for 30–40 minutes. Remove and leave in tins for 10 minutes. Turn out and cool on wire rack.

To make the syrup, heat all ingredients, except apricot jam, in a small saucepan, until treacle has melted. Make a few holes in cooled sponge bases with a fine skewer, and sprinkle syrup over. Sandwich sponges together with apricot jam.

To make the chocolate fudge icing, place all ingredients in a large

117

saucepan, and dissolve sugar over gentle heat. Bring to boil and continue boiling until temperature reaches 238°F (115°C) on a sugar thermometer (soft ball stage—small drop of mixture will form a soft ball when dropped into cold water and rolled with fingers). Remove pan from heat, set aside until cool, then beat mixture with a wooden spoon until thick enough to hold its shape. Spread over top and sides of cake. Leave for several hours to dry and then decorate as you want, or leave cake as it is—it is certainly rich enough.

Hallowe'en Spicy Hot Chocolate (*serves 4*)
This is a delicious warming chocolate drink spiced with cinnamon. Good on Bonfire Night too.

2 oz (50 g) plain cooking chocolate	Few drops of vanilla or almond essence
¼ cup sugar	1 dessertspoon finely grated orange rind
3 cups milk	A little single or double cream
1 cup water	
1 cinnamon stick	

Melt chocolate in a basin over hot water. Put sugar, milk, water, cinnamon stick, essence and orange rind in a saucepan and heat slowly, stirring continuously to dissolve sugar. Pour hot melted chocolate into saucepan and stir well to mix. Bring to boiling point and, stirring all the time, simmer for several minutes. Remove cinnamon stick. Just before serving, stir in a little cream and if you want to be even more luxurious grate a little extra chocolate on the top. Serve in steaming mugs.

Hallowe'en Turnip Soup (*serves 6–8*)
When you have finished making your turnip lanterns don't throw the flesh away—make this delicious soup. It doesn't sound very grand, but it tastes much better than you might imagine.

2 oz (50 g) butter	Salt
2 oz (50 g) onions, chopped	Freshly milled black pepper
1½ lb (675 g) turnip flesh, cubed	½ level teaspoon nutmeg
2 oz (50 g) brown bread	Double cream
1 tablespoon olive oil	Watercress to garnish
2 pt (1·25 l) chicken or veal stock	

Melt butter in heavy saucepan. Add chopped onion and cubed turnip. Cover with piece of greaseproof paper and saucepan lid and 'sweat' vegetables gently over low heat until tender—about 25 minutes.

Meanwhile, cut brown bread, including crusts, into ½in (1cm) cubes. Fry in olive oil until crisp and evenly browned.

...ied bread cubes to vegetable mixture. Add cold stock and
...ntly for a further 20 minutes. Season with salt, pepper and
...ass through a sieve, mouli, or blender. Reheat if necessary.
...h a swirl of cream and a few sprigs of watercress.

...ie (*serves 6–8*)
...been enjoyed since Tudor times. The pumpkin was
...d fried with sweet herbs and spices, and then put into a
...vith sugar, beaten eggs and alternate layers of apples
...Pumpkin Pie along similar lines was introduced by the
...s in America, where it has become a national dish. In
...went out of fashion during the eighteenth century,
...: Hallowe'en feast.

...are scooping out your pumpkins to make lanterns,
keep the flesh for this delicious pie, which is very spicy and has a
lovely creamy topping.

FOR THE PASTRY:

8 oz (225 g) plain flour
Pinch of salt
2 oz (50 g) margarine
2 oz (50 g) lard

2 tablespoons caster sugar
Finely grated rind of 1 lemon
1–2 tablespoons cold water

FOR THE FILLING:

1 lb (450 g) raw pumpkin
Pinch of salt
4 oz (125 g) soft brown sugar
½ teaspoon ground cinnamon
½ teaspoon ground ginger

¼ teaspoon ground nutmeg
1 tablespoon thick honey
2 eggs, beaten
Grated rind of 1 lemon
Grated rind of 1 orange

FOR THE TOPPING:

¼ pt (150 ml) double cream
Syrup from stem ginger to
 sweeten

¼ teaspoon ground ginger
2 oz (50 g) walnuts, roughly
 chopped and toasted

To make the pastry, sift flour with salt into a bowl. Add margarine
and lard in pieces and rub into flour with fingertips until mixture
resembles fine breadcrumbs. Stir in sugar and lemon rind and
enough cold water to bind mixture together. Form into a ball and
chill in refrigerator for at least 30 minutes.

When ready to use, roll out pastry on a floured board and line a
deep 8in (20cm) pie plate or flan tin. Set oven at 375°F (190°C)
Gas Mark 5.

To prepare filling, first cut up pumpkin flesh, removing seeds,
and stew gently in a little water until tender, about 15 minutes.
Strain and mash.

Mix together salt, sugar, spices, honey, lemon and orange juice and add beaten eggs, followed by grated lemon and orange rind and mashed pumpkin. Pour mixture into prepared pastry case and bake in pre-heated oven for 45–55 minutes, or until a knife inserted in filling comes out clean. Allow to cool.

To make the topping, whip cream, sweeten with ginger syrup and add ground ginger. Just before serving, cover pumpkin pie with this cream and sprinkle with chopped, toasted walnuts.

Pumpkin Soup (serves 6)

This warming Hallowe'en soup can be made from the flesh of the pumpkins you are making into lanterns. Serve steaming hot.

1½ lb (700 g) pumpkin flesh	Salt
1 oz (25 g) butter	Freshly milled black pepper
1 tablespoon plain flour	A little sugar to taste
1½ pt (750 ml) milk	¼ pt (150 ml) double cream
1 teaspoon basil	

Remove any seeds from pumpkin flesh. Cut into cubes. Cook in simmering water for 20 minutes, or until tender. Drain well. Pass through a sieve or mouli to make a purée.

Melt butter in a medium saucepan. Stir in flour and cook gently for a few seconds. Remove from heat and stir in milk to make a smooth sauce. Add pumpkin purée, and basil. Season to taste with salt, pepper and sugar. Bring soup to boil gently. Stir in cream just before serving.

Serve piping hot with sippets (cubes) of fried bread.

Soul-Cakes (makes 12)

In the last century it was customary to go 'a-souling' on All Souls' Day (2 November) or on All Saints' Day (1 November). Children used to chant a jingle as they knocked on people's doors begging for soul-cakes:

> Soul, soul, for a soul-cake,
> Pray good missus—a soul-cake,
> One for Peter, two for Paul.

These were in fact any gift given on these two days—fruit, drink, money or little plain or fruit buns. As you eat your soul-cake, you must say 'A soul-cake, a soul-cake, have mercy on all Christian souls.'

Good pinch of saffron	1 lb (450 g) plain flour
Warm milk	Pinch of salt
6 oz (175 g) butter	1 teaspoon mixed spice
6 oz (175 g) caster sugar	3 oz (75 g) currants
3 egg yolks	Milk to mix, if necessary

Pre-set oven at 350°F (180°C) Gas Mark 4. Soak saffron in a little warmed milk. Cream butter and sugar. Beat in egg yolks. Sieve flour, salt, and spices together and add to mixture. Lastly add currants and drained saffron milk. Add more milk if necessary, to make a soft dough. Make into flat cakes, mark each one across top, and bake on a greased baking tray in pre-heated oven for about 15 minutes or until brown.

Spooky Baked Apples *(serves 6)*

These are traditionally baked in cider with cinnamon. You can fill the cavity of the apples with dates, dried apricots, chopped glacé fruits, sultanas, raisins or anything you fancy. Serve hot on Hallowe'en.

6 large cooking apples	$\frac{1}{4}$ pt (150 ml) sweet cider
6 oz (175 g) demerara sugar	1 small cinnamon stick
Dried fruit (any kind)	3 oz (75 g) unsalted butter

Pre-set oven at 375°F (190°C) Gas Mark 5.

Choose firm, large cooking apples without blemishes. Wipe and core without going right through apple. Slit skin round centre of apple with a sharp knife.

Fill each cavity with some sugar and whichever dried fruit you choose. Place apples in an ovenproof dish with sweet cider and cinnamon. Top each apple with $\frac{1}{2}$ oz (15 g) butter and bake for about 40 minutes until tender. (Cooking time will vary with type of apple.) Baste once or twice with the juices in pan.

Serve hot with whipped cream or Spiced Wine Custard (see following recipe).

Spiced Wine Custard *(serves 6)*

This is a fifteenth-century recipe and is super with baked apples or any other fruit.

4 eggs	$\frac{1}{2}$ teaspoon ground mace
2 egg yolks	$\frac{1}{2}$ teaspoon ground cloves
1 pt (500 ml) red wine	A pinch of ginger, cinnamon,
2 oz (50 g) sugar	and nutmeg for sprinkling
$\frac{1}{2}$ teaspoon ground cinnamon	

Beat eggs and egg yolks. Heat wine and whisk into eggs. Mix in sugar and spices. Stir over low heat until thick. Pour into a serving dish. Sprinkle surface very lightly with ginger, cinnamon and nutmeg. Serve with Spooky Baked Apples (see previous recipe).

GUY FAWKES' NIGHT

Guy Fawkes' Night, 5 November, commemorates the failure of the attempt in 1605 by Guy Fawkes, Robert Catesby, Thomas Winter, Thomas Percy, John Wright, and others, to blow up King James I and the Houses of Parliament with gunpowder. Fireworks, bonfires and the burning of 'guys' are the main features of the celebrations.

Parkin, gingerbread and treacle toffee are traditional fare on Guy Fawkes' night, to be eaten around the bonfire. Jacket potatoes are cooked in the bonfire and served with steaming mugs of hot spiced drinks to warm the revellers on a cold November night.

Bonfire Toffee (*makes about 1¾ lb (800 g)*)
This is a lovely chewy toffee to get your teeth stuck into while you are watching the fireworks or standing round the bonfire.

1 lb (450 g) demerara sugar
¼ pt (150 ml) water
¼ level teaspoon cream of tartar
3 oz (75 g) butter

4 oz (125 g) black treacle
4 oz (125 g) golden syrup
Walnut halves (optional)

Brush a large shallow tin with a little melted butter and set aside.

Dissolve sugar in water in a large heavy-based saucepan over a low heat stirring occasionally. (Use the largest saucepan you have for making the toffee as this will help prevent the toffee boiling over.) Add remaining ingredients and continue heating gently until everything is mixed and sugar has completely dissolved. Increase heat and boil mixture rapidly until temperature reaches 270°F (132°C) or 'soft-crack' stage. (When dropped into cold water, the mixture separates into threads which become hard but *not* brittle.) Remove from heat and pour into prepared tin. Cool for 5–10 minutes, then mark into squares and, if desired, put a walnut half in the middle of each square. Leave until completely cold and set, then remove squares of toffee from tin and store in an airtight container.

Bonfire Toffee Apples (*enough for 10*)
Children, not to mention the grown-ups, love to eat these standing round the bonfire. They also look very festive if stuck into a decorated pumpkin or marrow for Hallowe'en.

10 small crisp eating apples	2 oz (50 g) butter
10 wooden sticks	4 oz (125 g) golden syrup
12 oz (350 g) soft brown sugar	1 teaspoon lemon juice
$\frac{1}{4}$ pt (150 ml) water	

Remove stalks from apples, and wash and dry them. Push a wooden stick into each one. Butter a baking tray or greaseproof paper.

To make toffee, put sugar and water into a heavy-based saucepan and heat gently until sugar is dissolved, stirring occasionally. (Have a bowl of cold water and a brush beside you to wash down any sugar granules which may stick to sides of pan as you stir.)

When all sugar is dissolved, add butter, golden syrup and lemon juice and stir until well blended. Increase heat and boil rapidly without stirring until toffee reaches a temperature of 290°F (145°C) or 'soft-crack' stage. (When dropped into cold water, it separates into threads which become hard but *not* brittle.) Remove from heat and allow bubbles to subside. Dip apples one at a time into toffee, making sure that they are completely covered. Twirl around for a few seconds to allow excess toffee to drip off, then plunge into a bowl of cold water. Remove and stand on prepared baking sheet or greaseproof paper (or an oiled marble slab if you have one) until set. If toffee begins to harden before all apples have been dipped, warm over a very low heat until liquid again.

Toffee apples may be stored wrapped individually in greaseproof or waxed paper, but *do* keep them in a dry atmosphere.

Guy Fawkes' Punch (*serves 10–12*)

2 tablespoons brandy
1 x 15 oz (425 g) can apricot
  halves, sliced
2 pt (1·25 l) red wine
3 tablespoons port

2 tablespoons dry sherry
½ pt (250 ml) water
1 cinnamon stick
12 cloves

Mix together brandy, sliced apricots and apricot juice. Put wine, port, sherry, water, cinnamon and cloves into a saucepan and bring slowly to boil. Add brandy and fruit mixture and serve steaming hot.

Spicy Mulled Cider (*serves 8–10*)

2 tablespoons soft brown sugar
Pinch of salt
4 pt (2·25 l) dry cider
1 teaspoon whole allspice berries

Large pinch of grated nutmeg
2 in (5 cm) piece of cinnamon
  stick
1 orange

Mix brown sugar, salt and cider together in a saucepan. Tie allspice and nutmeg in a square of muslin, and add to cider with cinnamon stick. Bring slowly to just under boiling point. Add twists of orange rind and a slice of orange when serving. Serve in earthenware mugs.

Spicy Tomato Soup (*serves 6–8*)
This is a lovely warming spicy soup to enjoy on Guy Fawkes' Night while standing round the bonfire. Serve it with tiny cubes of hot lemon-flavoured fried bread.*

2 oz (50 g) butter
2 oz (50 g) onion, finely chopped
1 sprig fresh rosemary or
  1 teaspoon dried rosemary
  or 1 bouquet garni
1½ oz (40 g) flour
¾ pt (400 ml) chicken or
  turkey stock

2 oz (50 g) tomato purée
Soft brown sugar to taste
1 pt (500 ml) tomato juice
1 blade of mace
1 clove
½ teaspoon paprika
½ wineglass port
¼ pt (150 ml) double cream

Melt butter in a heavy-based pan, add onion, put lid on pan and 'sweat' onion until transparent. Add rosemary or bouquet garni and flour and stir well. Add stock gradually, working soup with a whisk until smooth. Stir in tomato purée, sugar, tomato juice and spices. Cook gently for 20 minutes and strain. Just before serving add port. Reheat soup, and add cream. Serve immediately.
*Note: To make lemon flavoured fried bread, melt some butter in a frying pan and fry cubes of white or brown bread until golden brown. Add dash of lemon juice to pan and a sprinkling of salt. Stir to combine, and serve in soup bowl with the soup.

Sticky Bonfire Gingerbread (*makes about 12 pieces*)
This is a dark, spicy gingerbread which is delicious eaten on Guy Fawkes' Night to keep out the cold. Serve cut into thick wedges with steaming mugs of hot chocolate or mulled spiced cider.

6 tablespoons milk	Pinch of nutmeg
½ level teaspoon bicarbonate of soda	Pinch of mace
	Pinch of coriander
4 oz (125 g) unsalted butter	2 teaspoons ground ginger
4 oz (125 g) soft brown sugar	1 egg, beaten
6 oz (175 g) black treacle	1 teaspoon grated orange rind
8 oz (225 g) plain flour	1 teaspoon grated lemon rind
Pinch of ground cloves	2 teaspoons candied peel,
Pinch of allspice	chopped

Pre-set oven at 300°F (150°C) Gas Mark 2. Grease and line a 7in (18cm) square cake tin with greaseproof paper. Brush the inside with butter.

Warm 1 tablespoon of milk and dissolve bicarbonate of soda in it. Melt butter, sugar, treacle and remaining milk in a saucepan without letting it become too hot. Stir continuously while melting, then let it cool slightly while you prepare dry ingredients.

Sift flour and spices into a bowl and make a well in centre. Pour in beaten egg, then all other liquid ingredients, adding dissolved soda last. Mix thoroughly adding the grated and candied peels. Pour mixture into prepared tin and bake for about 1¼ hours or until well risen and springy.

Allow to cool for 10–15 minutes in tin before turning out on to a wire cooling rack. Remove greaseproof paper and leave to cool completely. Store in an airtight tin for at least 2 or 3 days before cutting.

Yorkshire Parkin (*makes about 12 pieces*)
This is a gingerbread speciality containing treacle and oatmeal, which is still baked in Yorkshire for Guy Fawkes' Night. By the late eighteenth century, treacle consumption was much higher in the North of England than in the South, because it was a cheaper sweetener than the refined white sugar, and the North was a poorer area. Oatmeal was also a cheaper cereal, so it is not surprising that parkin was developed.

Parkin is dark, heavy and spicy and good when eaten standing around the bonfire on a cold, dark night. A popular Yorkshire custom is to serve wedges topped with stewed apple.

8 oz (225 g) wholemeal or
  plain flour
½ level teaspoon salt
1 or 2 level teaspoons ground
  ginger
1 level teaspoon ground mace
1 level teaspoon ground nutmeg
6 oz (175 g) medium oatmeal
1 oz (25 g) soft dark brown sugar

4 oz (125 g) black treacle
4 oz (125 g) golden syrup
2 oz (50 g) margarine
2 level teaspoons bicarbonate
  of soda
8 fl oz (180 ml) warm milk
1 egg, lightly beaten
4 oz (125 g) seedless raisins,
  (optional)

Pre-set oven at 325°F (170°C) Gas Mark 3.

Sift flour, salt and spices together into a mixing bowl. Stir in oatmeal and sugar. Gently melt treacle, golden syrup and margarine over a low heat. (To measure treacle and syrup, weigh a small basin empty and then add treacle to basin and weigh again.) Make a well in centre of flour mixture and pour in melted ingredients. Dissolve bicarbonate of soda in warmed milk and add to mixture with lightly beaten egg. Add raisins if these are being used. Mix to a soft batter and pour into a lined and greased meat tin about 10 x 8in (15·5 x 20cm). Bake in pre-heated oven for 40 minutes. When cooked, parkin should be an even brown colour and have shrunk away slightly from sides of tin. Leave to cool on a wire rack.

If possible, keep parkin in an airtight tin for at least a week before serving. This way it will become much more moist and sticky. Originally it would have been kept in special wooden parkin boxes.

INDEX